# The Facets of Man
# Volume 1
# The Building Blocks

**Derrick Hodge**

VIKING SHIP PUBLISHING

P.O. Box 24577

Fort Worth, TX 76124

Copyright © 2011 by Derrick Hodge

All rights reserved, including the right to reproduce this book or portions thereof in any form whatsoever. For information, address Viking Ship Publishing Subsidiary Rights Department, P.O. Box 24577, Fort Worth, TX 76124.

First Viking Ship Publishing hardcover edition 2012

For information about special discounts for bulk purchases, please contact Viking Ship Publishing Special Sales at 682-559-1420 or facetsofman@yahoo.com

For more information or to book an event, contact the Viking Ship Publishing Speakers Bureau at 682-559-1420 or visit our website at http://www.facetsofman.com

Manufactured in the United States of America

10 9 8 7 6 5 4 3 2 1

Library of Congress Cataloging-in-Publication Data

**ISBN:** 978-0-615-62969-8

**ISBN:** 978-0-615-59099-8 **eBook**

First of all, I would like to give all thanks to God. I give him the praise for instilling a vision in me and opening the doors to allow for me to put my vision in motion. I would also like to thank James and Lucille, my parents. Without you, I wouldn't have existence. May you rest in peace, dad. To my daughter Derrian, you're my world. You are the reason for my everyday grind. Daddy loves you!

To Grandma Willie, thank you for showing me strength and determination. Through all of your hard times you still stayed positive and continue to keep pushing. To my wife Sylvia, thank you for putting up with the long days and nights while I worked on my vision. Love you! To the Viking Crew, Cory and Kirvin, true friendship lasts a lifetime! No matter how old you get.

To all of those that helped me along the way whether it affected me in a positive or negative way, it groomed me for the moment at hand. Without you, I would not have made it. I would not have endured. Thank you!

# Table of Contents

**Introduction**

**Part One: The Corrective Process**

Chapter 1 Accepting the Leadership Role as a Man

Chapter 2 Building a Home

Chapter 3 Where Are My Role Models

Chapter 4 Without Trust We Have Nothing!

Chapter 5 Peace of Mind

Chapter 6 It's More Than Money

Chapter 7 Appreciation

Chapter 8 Choosing Your Battles Wisely

Chapter 9 Celebrating Yourself

Chapter 10 Help! I Need My Altar!

Chapter 11 Come On! Where's Your Pride?

Chapter 12 Humility

## Part Two: What's Your Motivation?

Chapter 13 Give Me A Plan

Chapter 14 Submitted To The Plan

Chapter 15 When Okay Isn't Good Enough

Chapter 16 Outgrowing Your Circle

Chapter 17 The Pruning Process

Chapter 18 Bondage

Chapter 19 Psalms 1:1-3

Chapter 20 Adversity

Chapter 21 Men Cry in the Dark

Chapter 22 Let It Go!

Chapter 23 You Know Better

## My Pledge

# *Introduction*

The book that I present to you is titled The Facets of Man Vol. I: The Building Blocks. Let's define a facet. A facet is any one of the flat surfaces or angles cut into gemstones which are normally cut in order to improve their appearance by allowing them to reflect light. So, metaphorically speaking, I applied this same logic towards the man. You have different sides to you that make you valuable. Every circumstance that you went through in life just chiseled another facet into you to make you what you are today. After all, you are a gem right? Every single thing had its own individual purpose. They meant it for evil by tearing a piece of you away, all the while not knowing they were only increasing your brilliance.

You are a natural resource that is heavily sought after. They don't have to find you in a mine or at the center of the Earth. You're right here at the local store, at the gym, heck, on the third pew at church on Sunday.

Though you may come in different colors, you are still gems. Your brilliance comes from the amount of light that passes through you when every facet or angle is in perfect alignment. The previously stated line says your brilliance comes from the amount of light that is allowed to pass through you when you are perfectly aligned. Again, every single thing that for the moment, sliced a piece of you away, was just shifting and positioning you right where you needed to be, which was in the presence of the Everlasting light.

To your foes: The more they inflicted you, the more brilliant you became. The more they tormented you, the more exposed you became to the light. Now look at them! As you are now brilliant in the light, you're now considered a luxurious resource by their standards. It's funny, how at first, they just saw you as a clump of coal or a dirty rock but buried deep inside you knew what you were. They just couldn't see it beneath your rough outer coating. You were passed over in sought of the already polished gem. The funny thing, the already polished gem turned out to be a cubic zirconium. It was once said, "Never judge a man from his beginnings." "Judge him at his ending." Too bad, guess they missed out. Though you started rough, you knew who you were and to WHOM you belong. You believed in the vision that was already laid out for you. It was your job to keep the faith and pursue it. So now, as you are being held in HIS hand up to the light, He is pleased with you. You are welcomed with a, "Well done my child." "I knew you had it in you the whole time." "It was just up to YOU to dig deep within yourself and see the gift I planted within you." YOU ARE MAN!

# Part I

# The Corrective Process

## *Accepting the Leadership Role as a Man*

**1** Here is a trustworthy saying: If anyone sets his heart on being an overseer, he desires a noble task.
**2** Now the overseer must be above reproach, the husband of but one wife, temperate, self-controlled, respectable, hospitable, and be able to teach.
**3** He must not give in to drunkenness, not violent but gentle, not quarrelsome, not a lover of money.
**4** He must manage his own family well and see that his children obey him with proper respect.
**5** If anyone does not know how to manage his own family, how can he take care of God's church?
**6** He must not be a recent convert, or he may become conceited and fall under the same judgment as the devil.
**7** He must also have a good reputation with outsiders, so that he will not fall into disgrace and into the devil's trap.
**8** Deacons, likewise, are to be men worthy of respect, sincere, not indulging in much wine, and

not pursuing dishonest gain.
**9** They must keep hold of the deep truths of the faith with a clear conscience.
**10** They must first be tested; and then if there is nothing against them, let them serve as deacons.
**11** In the same way, their wives are to be women worthy of respect, not malicious talkers but temperate and trustworthy in everything.
**12** A deacon must be the husband of but one wife and must manage his children and his household well.
**13** Those who have served well gain an excellent standing and great assurance in their faith in Christ Jesus.
**14** Although I hope to come to you soon, I am writing you these instructions so that,
**15** If I am delayed, you will know how people ought to conduct themselves in God's household, which is the church of the living God, the pillar and foundation of the truth. − **(1 Timothy 3:1-15)**

## Building a Home

What does a home represent to you? Does it represent a sense of stability? Is it a safe haven for you? Is it a place of refuge where you can lay your head? What is your definition of a home? Now that you have taken the time to provide a defined answer for yourself, let's take a moment to discuss. The subtitle of this book is called, "The Building Blocks." I chose this subtitle because I feel that as a person, your life will be similar to building a home. My purpose for this book is to assist you with some of the building blocks that I feel it will take to build yourself up similar to building a home.

As you receive each building block, I suggest to you that you may be adding another piece to yourself further strengthening your foundation. I mention strengthening the foundation because everything in your life from birth will stem from your own personal foundation. When you research a house you see that the most important phase of the home building process is the building of the foundation. Why? Everything rests on it.

## "Everything in your life from birth will stem from your own personal foundation."

Since everything rests on the foundation it's no question that it is the most important part of the home. You, being the man of your house must be the foundation of your home. There is no hesitation about it. Everything that takes place in your home must be held together by YOU. If your foundation is not built properly you can't expect for your house to be in proper order. You can't look to her or the kids. It's not their design to have to assume that responsibility. God didn't appoint Eve as the foundation for mankind. He chose Adam. Guess what? Adam's a male. Stop putting all of the foundational tasks on your woman. Man up!

As I continue to go further, as a man, I should now have your attention. You should now be fired up and ready to go. That is, if you're in the proper role in your home. When God created Adam He gave all of the responsibilities to Adam. Eve wasn't even created yet. Therefore, you have no room for excuses. I feel my God given purpose is to enrich our males with building blocks to assume Adam's position. I want to start by addressing some of the building blocks it will take to strengthen your core. This is the pre Eve stage before your woman and the kids even came into the picture. If you're already past the pre Eve stage I hope to strengthen you with these building blocks as a chiropractor would do one's spine. Gently easing each piece into their proper alignment until you're able to stand upright and walk firmly as a man! Most importantly, as the core of your home!

A foundation could be defined as the basis or groundwork of a thing. I suggest to you that what your internal core consists of will spill over into your family. That's why it's very important that if you are thinking about assuming the role of "head of household" make sure that your core values are intact. Your household will ultimately come to you for the final say so on decision making. There are several men that walk around stating, "This is my house!" Well, is it?

Have you ensured that you have yourself together internally to wear the "big boy" pants? How many times have you driven past a finished home and seen the foundation? You're right. You haven't. You want to know why? It doesn't have to be seen to be the most important part of the home! The foundation of a thing has a sense of confidence in knowing and not showing that it is the almighty piece of the puzzle! So, I suggest that there is no need to have to walk around boasting to everyone that you are the man of the house. If you have it on lockdown everyone on the inside and outside will see it from looking at your household. When you have random people coming up to you stating that they see the unity and love in your home, you're doing the right things. That means you are headed in the right direction.

What I would like to do is take the moment to discuss a few of the traits that I feel may be helpful in strengthening your personal foundation as a man.

**Strength:** The quality of being strong

To be the man of the house there is no doubt that you must be strong for your home. When the going gets tough because it will, you must stand planted digging your feet into the dirt and be the rock for your house. You must stand in the gap and protect your home.

**Character:** The quality of having morals

To be the man of the house you should have high morals and values. What the world is trying to portray to you is a lie! Don't follow the world, follow your Godly principles. If you know it's wrong and will affect your home don't do it. What happens in the dark will come to the light. It's been proven every time.

**Resolve:** The act of making up one's mind, coming to a determination or transform by a mental process

To be the man of the house you should be a man of great resolution. You should always be the thinking force in your home transforming it by processes. This is where your relationship with God comes into play. After all, He is the Great Architect. Your blueprint or design for your home should be through Him. To be the head, you should be open to hear Him for resolution. Your wisdom should come from Him as you relay it and shape your home. Once heard from Him, you should have the final say in your home. You should be the navigation system for your home directing it in the proper direction.

**Faith:** The act of having trust in someone or something

We live by faith and not by sight. **2 Cor 5:7**

To be the man of your home you must be a man of great faith. You must know that everything is part of the plan that God has for your home. You must believe that no matter what, God has your back. When you go through a storm your faith in

God should bring you through. Though you may not see Him in the storm, He's there. You can't live by sight or what you see now. You must have faith that it will get better. Sight is the enemy of vision. Don't believe in what you see now. Also, being the man, you should have a faithful vision for your home. You should be the faith warrior for your home. When everyone else in your home gets weary you should still have great faith.

**Loyalty:** The act of being faithful to commitment

To be the man of your home you should be faithful and committed to your role as the head of your home. You can't straddle the fence to see what happens. You're either are all the way in or all the way out. Your home needs you to invest your all into being the foundation. If everything rests on you, you can't be faulty or your home will come tumbling down. Your family needs you to be solid in place if a home is going to be built upon you.

Of course, those are not all of the traits needed nor did I define them to the fullest but I wanted to point out a few great ones to start with. Everything here and throughout this book is to assist you with building your core values. Your core values will be your foundation for how you live your life. Just about everything that takes place in your life points back to your foundation. The decisions you make. How you view your relationships with other people. How you view your family life. How you view your future. They all point to the core which is your foundation. If your core is not in tact you may be in for a world of trouble. You could find yourself wasting a lot of useful time trying to patch up something you should have solidified in the beginning stages.

Let's explore the next phase. Using the same metaphor of building a home, the next phase of building yourself up is the building of your framework. The framework of a home is the portion of the home that rests on top of the foundation. It outlines the foundation and provides those on the outside a glimpse of how the home will be shaped. Though it may not be fully completed, the outsider can get their first glimpse of what's to come. The framework reveals the intricacies of the design. It reveals the dimensions of the home as a whole along with the dimensions of each room. The outsider could get a pretty good idea of the character of the home just from viewing the framework.

Let's apply this logic towards you. Going back to what was previously stated. In order to build yourself up properly you must ensure that you have a solid foundation since after all; you will be building everything on top of it. The framework of something can be defined as a set of ideas or principles that provide an outline. Simply put, your framework could be defined as your way of thinking. How you view things. How you react to things.

So you must have a solid "core" or foundation to impede you from having a distorted set of ideas or principles that will ultimately provide an outline for your life. This is where all of the preparation in building your foundation comes into play. No one perhaps saw the building of your foundation but they can see the building of your framework. Each piece is visible for the outside world to see. So now you have become exposed. Did you do diligence in preparing your foundation?

Let's explore some of the things your framework will reveal. A person on the outside should be able to tell the intricacies of your spirit by looking at your framework. If your spirit is not right within it will reflect on the outside. It will eventually be revealed for the outsider to see. The framework also reveals the character of a home hence revealing the true character of you. The way you conduct yourself in public can reveal your framework. The way you react to things can reveal your framework. Most importantly, the way you view things could reveal your framework. It all points back to who you really are and what you are all about. By the way, who you really are and what you are all about stems from your core values. Your characteristics were birthed by your core values. Reminding you again to ensure you have a solidified core.

A person should be able to tell where you are going by looking at your framework. I even suggest to you that you could associate a home's dimensions with a person's intellect and vision for themselves. The larger the home, the larger the capacity will be. If you have a shack sized mental capacity, guess what you will get? A shack sized outcome. You must blow the top off of the roof when it comes to your mental capacity. Remove the limits!

Though God may be the ultimate architect, you are the Earthly architect. Your ambition and tenacity alone could expand your personal framework causing you to have a larger playing field. Let's touch on the ambition part of it. Each piece of timber that has been laid is just another piece of the puzzle shaping you into an eventual finished product. Though you may view a nail as a sign of affliction, the Architect just views it as progress while He views the blueprints. One could view it as the shaping of something great. Be warned! You should never allow anyone to come in and place a board where there should not be one. You should never let anyone persuade you into halting your building process. The building must continue according to the blueprints.

Something to be truly mindful of is that everything associated with your framework will trickle down throughout your home. So the set of ideas or principles you may have, they will be spread throughout your home. So yes naturally, if they are good, your house will permeate goodness. If your principles are bad, your house will reflect it. So, don't look around at anyone else in your home. Check YOUR principles.

As the man of your home, your ideas should not stunt growth, they should promote it. Your principles should not discourage, they should encourage. The way you view things and react to things should not be detrimental to the framework of your home. So, as a man, your dimensions should be unmatched. The intricacies of your heart and spirit should be seen throughout the inside of your home as well as the outside. Every board should be in place and you should stand firmly while knowing that each nail is only part of the plan! Should I dare remind you of Jesus on the cross? Every nail may have been seen as an affliction but it was just part of the plan God had laid out! Continue to build!

So now we have this elaborate structure with all of these twists and turns but it is missing something. The home is starting to look as dapper as ever yet you have nothing to protect it all. The third phase in the building process is the building of the roof. The roof can be defined as the covering of a structure. It could also be defined as the highest point or the summit. Now that you have strived to ensure you have a solid foundation and solid framework, you must now be covered.

The roof covers and protects you from all of the outside elements. I must point out that outside elements are not to enrich you but to damage you. You picture a house. If it had no roof, what would rain or snow do to what's inside? You've guessed it. Everything would be destroyed. All of the man hours put into making something so special would all be in vain. The same applies to you. If you leave yourself exposed to the outside elements, everything that you have invested in would be in vain. I'm not a pastor nor am I ordained but I do suggest to you that you should allow for God to be your roof.

Going back to the definition of a roof, the roof can be defined as the highest point. With God you can't get any higher. Though some try, even ourselves at times, we all fall short. Everything in life happens for His purpose and not yours. You can even look at your birth for the confirmation. You were conceived and born to carry out His purpose for your life. You think about it. Out of all of those millions of sperms he chose one which turned out to be YOU. You were hand-picked. Though some of us may have been unplanned, it wasn't unplanned for God. So, fast forwarding all of the way to the present, you have a purpose. So stop living your life as if you don't have a purpose because you do or else you would not have been conceived. Live with purpose! Live according to God's blueprint for your life.

The problem several of us have is that we forget God has the blueprint and not us. Our foundation was laid out by Him. We just choose to mess it up by not following His blueprint and trying our own. That's why it's so hard to repair! The core values that we display in our homes as well as the framework on the outside are from Him. He knows the blueprint. He knows what boards belong and which ones don't. The most fascinating thing is that he has placed a blank check in our hands. As long as we follow Him, our capacity could be as large as we want it to be. It's all in how large we allow our capacity to become. The blank check represents that He will provide all of the resources we need abundantly so there is no limit to what we can attain. It's all on YOU!

All of this comes back to allowing for God to be your roof. Allow Him to fend off the outside elements. The hail, the snow, and the rain all will fall short to the roof. After all, He did create the elements in the first place. Therefore, what elements do affect you were allowed with a purpose in mind. The elements weren't meant to destroy you. They were meant to add to the design. Guess what? Remember that "faith" I spoke of previously in the chapter? Your faith can be represented as your insurance claim! If you have faith in Him, you will have full coverage! This means you have to pay nothing out of pocket yet you are restored. How great is your FAITH?

Going from the spiritual realm to the Earthly realm you are also part of the roofing phase. As the man, you must also be the summit of your home. There should be nothing higher in your home but God. You should take on the roles of leader, teacher, delegator, provider, protector, peacemaker and spiritual warrior. Though that doesn't encompass all of them, those are some of the heavy hitters. You should be the compass for your home. They should know what direction you all are going. Being the compass allows the time to teach what turns to make and which ones not to make.

Taking on the role of the delegator allows for you to assign what role is best for each person to flourish. Being a provider allows you time to show that if you follow me I will nourish you. Being a protector allows you the time to show that no weapon formed against the home will prosper. Being a peacemaker allows the time to expose the fact that you impede progress if there is no peace. Most importantly, being a spiritual warrior allows the time to show that God has your back and it is all part of the plan to build your home!

I must say that for everyone who took the time to read this chapter and the time to read the building blocks throughout this book, I'm praying for you. I'm praying for you to be restored as an individual. We all have fallen short in some areas.

We all have made mistakes. The great thing is, as long as we have breath in our lungs, we have a chance to correct them. God gave us another chance. It's only over when your clock stops so seize every moment of your life to be the best individual you can be. Believe me when I say, "It's contagious!"

Stop letting the world dictate you. You dictate it! Build your home the right way. Build yourself up the right way! If you aren't stable you can't expect for those around you to be stable. Your stability is contagious whether it's inside of your home or not. Make forth the effort to re-evaluate your core values. Though it may be difficult to do, remember, the rest of your home is relying on you to! They are relying on a better you! Build on!

## *Where Are My Role Models?*

"Keep my requirements and do not follow any of the detestable customs that were practiced before you came and do not defile yourselves with them. I am the LORD your God."

**Leviticus 18:30**

**Role Model**: Someone worthy of imitation. A person who serves as an example whose behavior is emulated by others.

Now ask yourself. **"Are you a role model?"**

    Role models are a very essential part of anyone's life. They are the people that you look up to. They're the people you emulate. Of course they're important in your lives. Role models can come in all shapes and sizes but ultimately they have two effects on you. A role model's effect could be a positive one or it could be a negative one. It all depends on the way it is presented by the role model and how it is received by the pupil. Being in the role of role model has its perks but most of all it holds its challenges. I mean that from a personal level as well as a teaching level.

On a personal level, being a role model holds its challenges from the obvious. You have someone looking up to you. That alone could bring pressure in itself. When you assume the role of role model whether or not you agree, you're automatically placed on a higher pedestal. You are forced to be mindful of every move or action that you take due to the fact someone else is watching.

If you are out to have a positive effect on your pupil you may be forced to do away with some of the seemingly detrimental habits you had before. You may be forced to stop drinking or to stop smoking. Perhaps you can't go to the same places you used to go. You are forced with the realization that the path you choose to take may ultimately affect someone else's life. You have to be careful because I'm sure you don't want the guilt if it ends up being in a negative way.

Let's switch to the challenges within for a role model when it comes to being a teacher. First of all, if you assume the role of a role model you must be a great teacher. You must be able to articulate yourself effectively so that it comes across to your pupil in the correct way you intended. You must ensure that your pupil understands completely with no hesitation the point you are trying to drive home. If not, things could be taken out of context which could turn out badly. Another challenge that could be faced is standing behind your teachings.

Don't tell your pupil not to do something and then turn around and do it yourself. You may then be considered a hypocrite by your pupil which is one of the worst things possible as a teacher. Once you have become a hypocrite, you possibly have lost your pupil for good because at that moment trust has been broken. You must realize that your pupil not only looks up to you but they have placed their trust in you as well. You literally could be holding their future in the palm of your hand. That's why you should be very careful before accepting this role. It holds great responsibility.

Let's switch to a more gender oriented approach. Let's address the effects of a male role model in a young boy's life. Although he may not have known it, your dad became a role model the day you were born. As young boys, we tend to gravitate towards our fathers because dad is the first relative being in our lives. Of course we had mom but with dad being of the same gender, we had more of a relation. Gender normally relates to gender. Emotions and mannerisms are relative. We could relate to what we saw dad do. We may not have known why at that stage in our lives but we could imitate what dad did naturally. That's why fathers are so important to young boys. Your son is trying to be you from the time he laid his infant eyes on you. This is what makes that particular time period so fragile. He can only do what he sees and can relate to, not what he knows at that point.

**"As young boys, we tend to gravitate towards our fathers because dad is the first relative being in our lives."**

With that being said, if you don't bother to stick around what are you leaving your son to emulate? Therefore, he does not know. The absence of dad leaves a huge void in a boy's life. He's left with no relative gender which could lead to a sense of emptiness. This could also lead to him struggling with his manhood as he grows older. We all know that an idle mind is the devil's workshop so this sense of emptiness could cause a young boy's life to go north or south. There is a reason there is an increase in femininity in the male gender today. There are fewer men who are sticking around to show these young boys what a man is supposed to do. These young boys are stuck to watch mom who's gender is a female. So naturally, they are growing up doing what they see and not what they know. The father that didn't care to stick around has created a confused young boy. So, to the fathers that left, "Blame yourselves for what you are seeing in our society today!"

In this scenario, as a young boy grows older, there's still a chance that he will be trying to fill the void of daddy not being there into his manhood. Until a young man has become comfortable within himself, he may also be in search of acceptance since he feels as if he were rejected at a young age by his father. This could very well be why there are an alarmingly high number of our young men today who are in and out of jail. They are performing the actions of trying to fill a void.

The normal reaction of trying to fill a void is an action of lashing out and the action of being indifferent. Dad wasn't there so why does it even matter? Internally, though it may be private, there is a bit of rage within them. That rage comes from not having a father figure there when they needed him the most. They have been left confused as to what a young man is supposed to do and how he should react in certain stages of his life. A future king can't become a king if he has no blueprint. He's left to waste countless years of being the court jester until he finds out who he is to become. Until he finds out the true greatness that runs through his veins! As a father, you call yourself so great, teach your children to be great. Strengthen your bloodline. It's all in the bloodline!

> **"A future king can't become a king if he has no blueprint."**

To a young male that feels as if he has nowhere to go, all of a sudden, the neighborhood gang mom always told him to stay away from may look a lot more attractive. A gang can be defined as a group that has close social relations. The gang provides a false sense of relation the young man has longed for since a young age. If the young man joins the gang that has welcomed him with open arms, the gang has now become his new role model. Though destructive to our society, all that is seen is a void filled not identifying the corruptive cycle that has just continued.

If you've sat down and had a conversation with at least 20 gang members, the majority of them may give you the same answer. Their answers would most likely be in reference to their fathers or lack thereof. Their actions and their current situation had something to do with their fathers. You want to move out of the neighborhood you're in because of the thugs hanging out on the street corners? You want to get out because of the high crime rate?

To the father that has left his son, "Where were you before he got to this point?" "Where were you when he needed direction?" You can't all of a sudden show up if he becomes wealthy! Where were you during the rough times; the times he needed you to help shape him into a man? You turn on the news and see a 16 year old boy wanted for manslaughter about to throw his life away. Gee, thanks dad! We lost another man since you felt the need to not care!

Let's switch gears and take a brief moment to touch on my situation coming up. I know everyone has their own situation but I do this in hopes that the reader better understands the seemingly little things that can affect a young boy's life. True, to the outsider, they may seem like little things but little things add up to be big things. My mom and dad were married at the time of my birth so I started off with dad there. As the early years went by, it abruptly came to an end prematurely.

I hadn't even begun 1st grade and my role model was out of the door and out of my life. One moment I was trying to emulate my dad and the next I was searching for answers. All I could remember is that day standing next to my mom in front of the old red courthouse in downtown Dallas waiting for my dad to show up. At the moment, I had no clue what was about to happen and how this would affect my life going forth. My parents were meeting to finalize the divorce.

At an early age, I had just lost the first relative role model in my life which was my father. How would I learn? Where would I go for those answers to life's challenges? Who could I emulate? I felt cheated. To this day, I still grapple with these feelings well into manhood. I still had a relationship with my father but it wasn't on an everyday basis. I saw him when I could.

I must point out that when you are younger and your dad has been snatched out of your life, the times when you do see him can cause you to not take it for what it really is. You tend to mentally and emotionally over exaggerate the situation because you want it to be so special. You find yourself fishing for anything so you can later look back at it as a memory. You want to cling to that brief moment as if it would be your last. Still young, I didn't know the magnitude of the situation but as I grew older, I got a better outlook on things. I'll never disrespect my father, but as I became a man I had to realize that daddy wasn't Superman. It was as though he had become subjected to his own personal kryptonite.

While younger, my role model looked closer to Superman but as I grew older I realized that he was more like Clark Kent. I realized that a role model could fall short. As I dissected it more I had to ask myself the questions, was my role model genuine? Was it forced or did my role model really care about where I was going in life? Did he care about how I would turn out? It goes back to what I stated previously, you have to be very careful when assuming the role of a role model. Although, in this case this was the father of a son, it still holds truth. Before you think of conceiving a child you must think long and hard because you will automatically become propelled into the role of a role model whether you like it or not.

As the pupil, you must digest what your role model has left you with in the proper way. It's not all on them even though they are the teachers. You have to work with what has been placed in your lap. I can honestly look back and say that I did digest what my father left me with in a negative way at times in my life. My perception of the short comings caused me to become a bit rebellious. I grew up in life going against the grain just because. It was a way for me to release my anger. I was confused and didn't have a clue as to how to handle the situations placed upon me so I just got angry.

Don't get me wrong I did have an older step brother. Maybe he would take over where dad left off? Not quite. He himself didn't have a male role model coming up either. Unfortunately, his dad had passed away at a younger age. This left two rebellious young men searching for someone or something to fill the void. If my older brother was searching for answers himself and I, being the younger was searching for answers in him, it's the blind leading the blind. Both of our situations led us through a destructive cycle. Several bad habits and demons that my brother had constantly battled with were being passed right down to me generationally due to him being the teacher and me trying to emulate him.

After a while, I had begun to resent everyone and everything around me. Resentment is a natural reaction when you realize that the person you had been looking up to all along had steered you in the wrong direction. One of the first thoughts that go through your mind is, "How could they do me like this knowing that I wanted better for myself." One thing I did have to learn is the old phrase. "Misery loves company." Some people can't accept how their lives turned out so they set out to recruit others to join their lifestyle, even if it is at the expense of someone else's future. I also learned that just because they may be a family member and assuming the role of a role model, they still have their own demons to fight as well. Being in the same bloodline does not make them exempt from their own personal battles. I picked up several bad habits but I don't blame my brother for any of my actions or the way I grew up. There is no blame to hand out here, only teachings for the reader.

My perception of it all at a young age allowed me to become a seed being injected with toxins. My original purpose was to grow into what I was meant to become. The only problem with that is I had not been fed the proper additives at that time in my life and I was malfunctioning. If you malfunction, you become destructive and you have a distorted perception. In that case you could find yourself living the rest of your life behind bars for a crime due to destructive behavior. You could find yourself being 40 still hanging out on the street corners with the gangs withering your life away. I had to uproot it! One of the most difficult things to do is to uproot something bad that has been planted within you.

To uproot something can be defined as to pull it up by the root. This reverts back to the core values mentioned in the previous chapter. The process of uprooting caused me to re-evaluate my core values and remove the ones that proved to be detrimental. Warning! Detrimental core values are like weeds. If you don't pull it by the root, they will come back. Therefore, do it right the first time. I can honestly say that I am now a better man due to my extensive uprooting.

I do want to point out one thing. This chapter is not all about the negative effect of a role model. There are several positive role models that are willing to step up to the plate instead of shying away to make a difference in someone's life. They may not have asked for it but they accepted the role anyway. This starts with dad. To all of the dads out there, all the way into manhood a positive father could mean a world of difference in a boy's life. He can relate to the thought of, "If dad is positive, I should be positive." "If dad is trying to do something with his life for him and the family, I need to do the same when I'm able to have my own home." Dad, just taking time out of your day to listen to what your child has to say is golden.

You may not realize it now, but your child will remember those moments for a lifetime. Whether it's looking at a scrambled Crayon picture from daycare or being in the stands of his football game. That picture stays in the brain for a lifetime and the image will be, "Daddy cared about me." There are several times in life that we may say we are too busy but in reality, we're not too busy for our kids. It's more of an excuse. I've lived this, been a part of this, and grew up going through this. Slow down a bit. Time with them is a precious commodity because they grow fast.

To this day, I still have fond memories of me being in the backyard with an old plastic football helmet and a football listening to my dad as he taught me the game. I remember standing in the dining room with him showing me the difference between a jab, hook, and an uppercut. Now into my 30's, those memories are still fresh in my mind.

Let me point out. You don't have to be the biological father of a child to make a difference either. Whether you are a step parent or you just took notice of a child who needed direction in their lives, you're making a difference. You have to think, these young boys out here are the future kings of this land. In a time where there's more emphasis placed on getting shiny wheels and seeing how low we can wear our pants, we need to be taking notice. We are at war here! We're losing our young men to violence. We're losing them to homosexuality. Our young men today need us more than ever! They need to be taught how to be a RESPECTABLE man.

This is a call to the older, more mature man. How about showing the younger men how to treat our women? Sad thing about it is that in this day and age, a lot of women have given up on men all together. They are tired of the games and being mistreated. There are women out there that have seen dysfunction for so long, that they feel as if that's just how all men are. They accept second class service when it should be first class. We, as a gender have exposed so many trifling acts to our women that they are conforming to them. Then, as a man, when you are ready to settle down, you become angry when you can't find a good woman. It has to stop!

No, we're not all perfect and it won't be perfect all the time but show that young man that is watching how to show some affection to a woman. If junior grows up seeing dad loving on mom, it's a great chance that he will grow up having similar traits. He will grow up viewing women with a sense of worth. Simple things you do from opening car doors, to surprising her with flowers every now and then help form his image of how things should be when it comes to a woman. Even the time he saw you pop mom on the backside playfully while she was in the kitchen cooking. The image of how dad treats mom is a huge thing. What he sees, he tries to become. Remember that.

To the young man out there, don't think you're too young to become a role model to someone else. With the billions of people in this world, there's always someone watching you. Get your mind right first. It starts in the mind. Every action starts with a thought first. If your mind is right, your actions will be right. I know society is trying to dumb you down by glamorizing this thug mentality. What's wrong with doing the right thing?

You can set an example just by wearing a belt around your waist and keeping your pants up. I'll be straight with you. I'm not saying I didn't go through that phase myself but my mother told me one thing that stuck with me to this day. "Always dress up to an interview no matter where it is and who it is for." The reason being, first impression means a lot.

You may aspire to become an entrepreneur when you get older. You can't walk into a board room to do business with your clothes hanging off of your bottom and tattoos everywhere. If you were on the other side of the table would you write a million dollar check to someone that didn't look promising or legit? It doesn't matter how qualified you are. You may have all kinds of degrees but your appearance could stereotype you. Conduct yourself presentably. Though you may not see, someone's watching you.

What I want to get out of reaching out to the youth is simple. "Each one, teach one." Though you are young, you still can teach your peers on how to make a positive impact. The older generation may not be able to reach them as effectively as you can. Your life may be more relative to what the youth may be going through at this point in their lives. The youth is our future. Becoming a role model or positive influence to an individual at a young age affects that individual for a lifetime. Let's not wait until our youth has battle scars and wounds before we lend a helping hand. You must start early in their lives. The earlier you start, the more aware they will be coming up of not going astray. Their view of life won't be of what they see just in their neighborhoods or what the television tries to tell them they are. Their view of life will be full of promise and purpose.

You must realize that you are holding the baton. Someone is looking up to you and you will be passing it right along to the next generation. Be responsible for the bettering of your environment and your society. It's all about taking the time out to teach. People who look up to you are like sponges. They want to soak up all you have to offer. Make sure you offer them something of value. Offer them something of worth.

For all role models, during the teaching phase become a counselor to them as well. Take the time to show them how to hone their God given abilities. More importantly, help them find them if they don't know how. Also, if you help someone find their gift, don't be afraid to help them harvest it. Put them in the best possible position for them to flourish. Teach them that potential is uncapped. Yes, there will be some rough times and they will turn to you for guidance. Be encouraged for them. Continue to fill them up when their tank runs empty. You have to be strong for them by standing in the gap between success and failure. I just ask one huge thing out of you. When you see them starting to become successful, never come at them with resentment or jealousy. You're not a role model if you despise the success of your protégé. You must stand back and be proud of your finished product. Think about where they could have been at this stage in their lives but you made the difference. To the role model, I salute you for your efforts. Your society thanks you!

## *Without Trust, We have nothing!*

Trust is one of the most important things in a relationship. It especially holds truth in this day and age with everything going on. To be honest, without trust, you don't have much. You might as well pack up your bags and call it a day. Trust is one of the core essentials when it comes to a relationship. Unfortunately, when you normally mention the word "trust" when it relates to a relationship, it portrays a woman's distrust in a man. It's plastered all over your television sets along with it being portrayed in the media. It makes it hard for a man from the beginning.

A lot of men seem to be the beneficiary of a horrible wrap when it comes to trust in a relationship. So much that a woman may state that she loves her man with all of her heart but she doesn't fully trust him. I'm sure the men know exactly what I speak of when I say this. We've all heard the phrase, "I trust you as far as I can see you." It's like going into a court room and the judge tells you that you are guilty until proven innocent. Where's the fair chance at proving yourself? There is none. Now, I'll admit that lack of trust may have come from a past experience that a woman may have had. She may have been hurt in the past and now it is extremely difficult for her to fully trust a man. On that note I ask the question. Why date if you don't fully trust me? Really, why go through all of the motions of playing like we are in a relationship and you don't fully trust me? You're wasting my precious time and yours.

### "A lot of men seem to be the beneficiary of a horrible wrap when it comes to trust in a relationship."

Now, I unfortunately have to admit that some men have broken the trustworthy bond in their relationships. This forces me to reference the relationship that may have experienced the male breaking that bond. I don't want to touch on the reasons why it took place. I just want to know, "Do you really want to be in the relationship you're currently in?" Don't waste her time by asking for forgiveness if you are not sure if it won't happen again. Go ahead and let her go. Let her find a man that is fully committed to her while you get yourself together. I know it's hard but you can't have it all. So many men want to keep the main squeeze at home while they run the streets. As a man, I must say, "That's not the way it is designed." You must make a decision. You owe it to her to be truthful to yourself.

I once heard, "Does a zebra change its stripes?" Yes, if the guilty party is truly apologetic and committed to correcting their errant ways. The question to ask is, "Will I get a fair shake going forth?" If you are in a relationship and you have tarnished your image with your lady, please realize there's a great chance going forth that you will not be fully trusted. She may have forgiven you but she does not fully trust you. No matter how much you try and even show her that it's nothing going on, deep inside her distrust still remains.

Let's take the following scenario for example. I'm sure some men can relate. Things could be going great between the both of you and your day could not be going any better. Something comes up which causes you to have a disagreement. For some time, she has been telling you how much she truly loves you and has all trust in you. The deeper you go into the disagreement, what does she do? You quickly realize that all of those loving words you've heard throughout the week were stated with a disclaimer. You have opened Pandora's Box and now she proceeds to bring up every mistake that you have made in the past. She may even go back years into her archives.

From a male's perspective, we may sit there a bit perplexed at what is unfolding right before our eyes. Our woman is rattling off things that were from the past and we had assumed that the issue was over. Wrong! It's almost as if your mistakes were your woman's ammo. She had locked it away in case of emergency, just in case she had to go to battle with you. When it got heated in your disagreement, she had reached into her bag of tricks and pulled out a bigger gun to go to battle with.

So, in this scenario I ask, "Is it worth it being in a relationship if you've broken the trust?" Think about it for a moment. You may never be trusted again. Although you may be on the straight and narrow she may do her best to keep you walking on eggshells. You two may never be the same again. So, I ask this particular male, "Was it worth all of this?" Was it worth stepping out and doing what you did? Five minutes of pleasure over here but a possible lifetime of torment depending on how long the relationship lasts.

Let's bring technology into the picture. Technology today has become one of the biggest killers of trust in a relationship, primarily cell phones. A cell phone is almost a sure fire way to tell if your woman trusts you or not. If you can get on your phone comfortably and not have any issues or questions, you may have a fighting chance. That means you may have a woman who is comfortable enough in herself and comfortable enough in you. Now, if she's not comfortable in herself, there may not be peace.

Each time your phone flashes, she will be making a mad dash to your phone as if the calls or text messages were meant for her. I know it could definitely put the man in a catch 22 situation. If you answer, she will be there to hear every spoken word, even if it's a friendly phone call. If you don't answer, it raises speculation with her as to why you didn't answer. The same goes for text messages.

Speaking of text messages, who has been in a situation that has you face to face with an obscene picture or gesture sent from an ex-girlfriend? Although it may not have been provoked and you had nothing to do with it, it always seems to wind up in the hands of the woman that you are currently in a relationship with. It never fails. For some reason, when we get something like that we don't delete it at that moment. We tend to want to enjoy the picture a bit longer which leaves us trying to explain ourselves later. I know someone out there can relate to this scenario. Women seem to not understand some of the issues that men go through when it comes to this sort of thing. They go by what they see and don't bother listening to the facts. Other women know that, which is why some ex-girlfriends will send these types of things in hopes of that scenario taking place. They want to sabotage your relationship in hopes of luring you back. What is a man to do?

The funny thing about all of this is that most men can care less about our woman's cell phone. They could stay on it for hours as much as we care. That just keeps them out of our faces for that time period. Which raises the question, "Why do the trust levels differ so much between women and men?" We put more trust in our women than they have for us although, being untrustworthy, does not have a specific gender.

Women can be very untrustworthy themselves. Men just make it easier for them so they rarely get caught. Mainly, this is due to men allowing women to have proper spacing. Now this doesn't mean all men go and raid your woman's cell phones. Although you should, just to make her a bit uneasy if there IS something she's hiding. I'm just joking. I'm merely just pointing out how the trust levels can differ between the two genders.

I close by pointing out the fact that trust is a vital part of a relationship. How can the both of you move forward together without it? Going into a relationship I feel that each person should leave their past situations behind them. Yes, I know that may be easier said than done but you must if you plan on giving your new mate a fair chance. You can't go into a relationship with one foot already straddling the fence, keeping an option open for the way out. Relationships are about entrusting someone with YOU. If one of the participants in a relationship is not willing to do that, don't bother going down that road.

To both parties: Think about how much it took out of you to entrust the other person in the relationship. As hard as each of you worked to gain the trust, why would you risk it all on a cheap thrill? Whatever the cheap thrill might have been was it worth it? I thought you would see where I'm coming from. Trust is such a delicate thing. You must handle it with care. If you handle it improperly, it could easily become tainted. Once tainted, it's like the BP oil spill. You will have a huge mess on your hands and it's going to take major time to clean up. Days, months, even years could go by with it not fully being restored. Be careful with someone's trust. Handle it with care because if you don't, you will truly have nothing.

## Peace of Mind

*"You will keep in perfect peace him whose mind is steadfast, because he trusts in you."* **Isaiah 26:3**

What does peace of mind mean to you? Take the proper time to mull it over and get a definitive answer that suits YOU. Now ask yourself, do you really have peace of mind? You may be surprised by your answer. The constant hustle and bustle of everyday life could put you in a state where you can't think or function properly. Whether being overworked in a 9 to 5 or ripping and running across town to take care of the house. Your mind is constantly working. Ever get to the point where you have to stop everything you're doing and say to yourself, "I'm burned out?" I know there may be some of you thinking, "I'm at that point now." You're slowly deteriorating mentally because you haven't allotted time for your mind to rest.

The problem is that most of us are so used to the hustle and bustle lifestyle we feel as though it's the norm. It has gone on for so long that we have become programmed as though we were robots. We've been blinded of the fact that we're human. We're not immortal. We will eventually break down from the wear and tear. It's similar to a pre-owned car. You shouldn't get so wrapped up on the outside appearance. You should be focused on the mileage. The mileage will indicate the usage of the vehicle and the value. The more mileage, the more chance you have of the car breaking down shortly after you drive it off the lot, in which case it loses its value. The same logic could be applied when it comes to the human body, particularly the brain.

The brain is the most complex organ in the human body. Although it may be complex, it still has its limitations and will wear down if abused. This is commonly referred to as being "burned out." What normally happens when you're mentally burned out? You can't think properly. You tend to make poor decisions. You're on edge for no apparent reason.

Warning! Being "burned out" can have its side effects. One of the most noticeable side effects is your lack of joy. You become so burned out that you lose a bit of your joy. You no longer act the same. You start to view the world from a melancholy state. Your emotions don't get too high and they don't get too low. It's almost as if you are depressed. You're just co-existing going along with what life deals you every day.

*"May the God of hope fill you with all joy and peace as you trust in him, so that you may overflow with hope by the power of the Holy Spirit?"* **Romans 15:13**

Another possible side effect would be the urge to lash out at your surroundings. Remember, in the mental state of being "burned out", your brain is desperately seeking relaxation causing it to gradually shutdown from the lack thereof. The lashing out occurs because you are not responding to what your body is trying to tell you. There is a struggle taking place from within. The battle is between your body and your will. All the while this battle is taking place; you're walking around with a chip on your shoulder.

The problem lies in the lack of reality that you still must interact with other people no matter what. So, due to this lack of reality, as soon as anyone says something to you, you lash out. Although it may be the smallest bit of interaction, you view it as the perfect opportunity to unleash all of your pinned up frustrations.

What did anyone do to you? What gives you the right to take your frustrations out on innocent bystanders? Who appointed you? The issue may very well be that you yourself may not even know the source of your sporadic behavior. You're just not yourself. The funny thing about it is when it becomes revealed to you of why you are acting this way; it doesn't have to be anything dramatic.

You can be riding in your car on the way home from work and it could just hit you. Now you are left to realize the foolishness of your behavior. God has a way of snapping you back into reality when you least expect it. Now you're forced to mend all of the valleys you have created with others around you because of your foolish outbursts. All from being "burned out."

Burning yourself out also brings a state of instability. This instability creates a yo-yo effect emotionally and mentally. Up and down your emotions go, never reaching a stable state. You never stopped to realize the core of your unstable behavior may lie in the fact you don't have peace of mind. You must stop and realize it's all a battle for your mind. Don't allow for your circumstances to blind you from seeing things clearly. Clear the clutter in your head!

It's not only circumstances that will make great attempts at your peace. There are people that if they had their way, you wouldn't have peace of mind at all. It's almost as if they are getting paid to attack your peace. Some people are so unhappy themselves that they want others to be in their state of chaos along with them. Remove yourself out of their presence if you can. The more you're in their presence the more of a chance their unhappiness has to seep into you.

Warning! Be cautious of those whom you were connected to in your past life. Once word gets out that you are on the road to peace and success, they will come out of the bushes and return in an attempt to re-connect. Don't look back! It's a reason the rearview mirror in your car is not bigger than your windshield. It wasn't meant for you to focus all of your attention looking backwards. It was meant for you to focus on moving forward. There was a reason you moved on in the first place or else they would not be your past.

Let's switch a bit and touch on the individual that purposely keeps himself overly occupied. You would rather do anything possible to keep yourself from relaxing. A lot of times when this happens, it's all an attempt to mask a deep insecurity that you have hidden within. You would rather focus on everything else instead of mind time. What are you running from? What you may not know is that you can't run from your mind forever. Like the overworked car, the parts began to wear out eventually. What will you do then? What will you do when you have overworked your mind and body so much that it is no longer functioning at a productive rate?

Last time I checked you can't trade in an overworked brain. I tell you one thing, seek God and deal with your insecurity. You may not like the exposure of your true feelings but you can trust your manufacturer. He made you, he has the instruction manual. You never know, your exposure just may give you back what has been missing in your life for all of these years.

My focus here was to make you mindful of your everyday routine. Does it allow for you to be as productive as you would like? Does your everyday routine allow you to "become?" I'll touch on "becoming" further in an ensuing chapter. Though you may not want to admit it, you know you have a bit of work to do. If you don't take the time to free your mind, no one else will. I pray peace over you! May God bring peace upon your mind, body and spirit! I pray that your mind allows for you to see the world as it were meant to be! I pray that whatever has your mind cluttered, that it dissipates allowing for you to have everlasting peace! Amen!

## *It's More Than Money*

What do you have to offer your woman besides money? Think about that with me. If you stripped away the finances and all of the fancy things you've bought her, would your woman still find value in you? Too many times as men, we dangle our financial successes in our women's faces if we are fortunate enough to make more than they do. This could be a problem as a lot of men become complacent and hang their hats on their finances. I must admit that it's a hard habit to break in this day and age when all you see is the "bling." Most men feel that as long as they pay the bills and put food on the table, that's all they have to do right? **Wrong!!!**

Although most of us may know this but not want to admit to it, women need more than our finances. I'm not suggesting that I know everything there is about what a woman needs but I have in my day been exposed to quite a few things they do need. I can tell you that a woman needs a friend. Have you ever been in a relationship and your woman viewed you as her best friend? If not, there may be something broke in your relationship. I say this because for the both of you to be in each other's presence 24/7, you have to be great friends. This world outside presents a hard enough challenge as it is and to not have a friend at home just compounds the turmoil. Ask yourself, how can you expect for her to be a help meet if you both aren't great friends? Would you go all out to help someone who you weren't friends with? You probably wouldn't.

## "A woman needs a friend"

Your woman needs a friend at home. I know men. There are times when you'd like to come in from a long day's work and jump right in front of the television to watch the game. Try taking a couple of minutes to at least see how her day went. Yes, you may be a bit inconvenienced for a while but think about it from her perspective. Women are very emotional beings. If you satisfy your woman's emotional side, you'll have her forever.

Besides, I'm sure if you ever had a rough day, you would want for her to stick around for a listen. You would want someone to vent your frustrations with. So, reciprocate the favor. Also, it's not all about the sexual aspect but when you get aroused at night, that couple of minutes you spent to satisfy her emotional side earlier that day, could make all the world of difference in your sexual experience. I don't have to elaborate.

I'm sure there are several men who know what I mean by the difference.

## "If you satisfy your woman's emotion side, you'll have her forever."

I would also like to suggest to you that you should assume the role of protector for your woman. Your protection should be a shield to her. That entails protecting her from the things she shouldn't be exposed to. I'm not saying that your woman can't handle herself, but some things are just different when you have two men handling business versus sending her to do business uncovered. One example of course would be the auto mechanic. She may only need one tire but she has let the mechanic persuade her into a whole new set of four. If you were there, things may have been different. You may have been able to see through the mechanic's ploy to increase the value of the sale.

## "Be a shield to your woman."

Let's also use the example of your woman shopping alone in the mall. Let's be honest men, we know ourselves. We know how other men could be when they see an uncovered woman. She may be hit on flirtatiously by all sorts of men, which could make her feel very uncomfortable.

Instead, why don't you accompany her more often so she could have a sense of security? I know, it may take her several hours to pick out something that may have been an in and out trip for you, but she now knows that she can walk in the mall freely without a care in the world. Next time you're out in public with your spouse, take note of how comfortable she is with you around. Her whole attitude will be different just by the thought of you being there. Though it may appear small to you, it speaks volumes to your woman.

Being a shield to your woman also means protecting her from those stressful situations. No matter how much she may put up the macho act, she still shouldn't have to be exposed to certain types of stress. She's not weak but she's fragile. That explains why the heart attack rate continues to increase in women on an annual basis. The gap that was once there between men and women pertaining to heart attacks has closed dramatically.

Not all, but a lot of this comes from the change in times. Women aren't just being home moms anymore. They are workers everyday just like we are. That means they are exposed to the same, if not, more stress than men go through on a daily basis. To top the work day off, a lot of the women are forced to come home and do another 8 hour shift of home tending. Men, we must start comforting and shielding our women more abundantly, which leads to my next topic.

Your woman needs love and romance. The woman lying next to you needs to know that you love her and that she is the only woman in your life. Loving her secures her and casts away any inhibitions that she may have. A woman that is loved will open up and be free. One thing I must point out. She will always give you what you are giving her. You give her problems; be prepared for her to give you problems back. You give her love; you will get love in return. You want a great woman, give her what she needs, which is the goodness of your heart. That goodness will be reciprocated by your woman.

By the way, chivalry is not dead men. Don't get so caught up in yourselves that you forget to be a gentleman. Put aside what it seems we are always hearing every time you turn on the radio or television. Your woman is not a "whore." She's your woman! The "B" word shouldn't be a regular part of your vocabulary. If you feel you have the need to call her these things then get ticked off at yourself. You're the one who made a poor choice of a woman. If you had a good woman treating you like the king you should be portraying, the thought of the word wouldn't even cross your mind. Also, if she allows you to address her in that manner, she's not the strong woman you need on your arm. She's handicapping you because she's not challenging you enough to assume the proper role of a respectable man.

## "Chivalry is not dead men."

It's nothing wrong with opening her car door from time to time. That's your woman! There is nothing wrong with surprising her with flowers at random. Take the time out to romance your woman. Take her out dancing, a walk in the park, to the lake. There's not enough of this going on in our relationships today which explains the steady increase in domestic violence. It explains the rise in our bitter women. It explains why you're a rarity if you are an affectionate and respectable man.

This is why you are the source of envy amongst her friends. They secretly are after her place in your relationship. Let them hate! It's nothing wrong with spoiling your woman from time to time. We as men always complain about our women keeping themselves up. Why not surprise her with getting her hair or nails done sometimes? You should want your woman to look her absolute best. She represents YOU. She's on YOUR arm, not anyone else's.

Doing these types of things will get into your woman's heart. That's the place you want to be when it comes to your woman. Most men know what I'm talking about. You get in your woman's heart, not her mind. Once you're in her heart there is nothing she won't do for you. She can always change her mind. Get it? Those of you thinking your sexual organ can cover the wool over her eyes have it wrong. What happens when your sex drive starts to decline? What are you going to do then? What will you have to offer her now? Exactly!

> **"You get in your woman's heart, not her mind."**

Let's address the area of leadership when it comes to your woman. No, she doesn't need to follow you around like a puppy dog, but your woman does appreciate great leadership in you. The both of you driving down the road undecided on where the both of you will eat is not too attractive to your woman. It actually shows a glimpse of weakness and it becomes quite irritating to her. When a woman meets you she views you as this strong leader type figure. Sort of like a man with a sword and shield in his hands. Work at maintaining that image that she has of you. If you don't, she may become less interested and seek leadership elsewhere.

Your woman really does want you to assume the leadership role. This means leading her into a secure environment and lifestyle. Taking charge and letting her know where the both of you are going in your relationship. Providing her with a plan and providing her with structure. Laying it all out on the table lets your woman know where the both of you are going and it gives her a fair chance to help you get there. If you don't let her know where the both of you are going, don't become irritated when she isn't meeting all of your needs. What she does not know, she can't help you with.

## "Where there is no revelation, the people cast off restraint; but blessed is he who keeps the law." Proverbs 29:18 NIV

Here, you see it from scripture. With no vision or sense of leadership, the people will cast off or perish. Be a leader to her. She will appreciate it. It actually takes a load off of her in just knowing you have it covered and mapped out. Most of the women that I have spoken with in my day appreciate not having to do it all by themselves. They appreciate a man coming in and assuming the leadership role. Take your place as the leader. A lot of men feel as long as they are bringing home the bacon, their women should be satisfied and say nothing. Yes, you should bring home the bacon but that's not the only thing that you should have to offer her. What happens if you lose your job tomorrow? Will you be able to sustain a healthy relationship?

Most importantly, will you be able to present yourself as the man of the relationship any further or will you consider yourself less of a man? If money is all that makes you feel like a man then you are mistaken. Broke or not, you should wake up every morning knowing that you are the man of your home. Being a man holds value in itself, what is money but merely paper? Provide more to your woman. Make yourself more valuable in the relationship besides handing out money. She should be calling you, "Daddy" for another reason, not because you have the "Sugar" in front of it.

## *Appreciation*

    This chapter is to address the act of appreciation. It's so easy these days to overlook the little things out of complacency with your partner. I hope by the end of this chapter you will develop a conscious effort when it comes to showing appreciation for your woman.

**"When I was a child, I talked like a child; I thought like a child, I reasoned like a child. When I became a man, I put childish ways behind me." 1 Corinthians 13:11**

How many times have you heard this quoted in reference to you growing out of your childish ways? Several times right? Whether it was a result of you doing something mindlessly in your adolescent state or something you did immaturely in your relationship, the majority of us you have heard this scripture. You maybe didn't want to hear it back then, but as you grew a bit older and wiser, boy, did that scripture ring true!

The way you act now should be totally different. Your thought process, should have taken a turn for the better. It's like when you were younger.

You may have jumped onto an amusement park ride with no recourse. Now, you may find yourself standing in line contemplating why you are putting yourself at risk by taking a three minute roller coaster ride. You now analyze before you make a decision about something because you know that one bad decision could set you back and time is not your friend.

Let's face it. You just grew up and became a man. Some circuits refer to it as, "Getting your grown man on." You even dress differently. Most of you have traded in the baggy jeans, for suits and ties. You've changed your thought process, dialect, and appearance which are great changes for a man coming into his own. Mainly, you are now showing a greater appreciation of yourself.

While showing a greater appreciation of yourself, how has your thought process evolved when it comes to your woman? Do you really appreciate her the way you should? Yes, I know some of you have shown the ultimate appreciation by getting married to her, but what about after the wedding? Did your appreciation for her go beyond the honeymoon stage? After the tuxedo and wedding dress has been placed in the attic, now what? Some of you have fallen into a complacent state. You see this person every day.

You know them inside and out. Besides, she now wears the rock you've spent a great deal of money on. She's not going anywhere and she should be grateful right? Not true! If you don't know by now, women like to feel needed. They like to know that they are still the sparkle in your eye. They like to know that they are still the same beautiful woman that you said, "I do" to. How else would you show them this? You should show them through appreciation of course.

Appreciation can be defined as an *expression of admiration*. Admiration could be defined as *delight*. So in terms, you are showing her that you are so delighted with her that you actually admire her. Ever catch yourself while your woman walked by just gazing at her? Sometimes you even have to add that little "grunt" with it. You know exactly what gaze I'm referring to so I'm sure you agree that it's indeed a form of appreciation. If you don't have that "grunt" with it no worries, read on. Hopefully by the end of this chapter it will come back to you.

That leads into the obvious topic in which I won't hang my hat on too long. Making love with your spouse is indeed a form of appreciation. The appreciation doesn't necessarily have to be the whole ordeal in the bedroom. The appreciation could very well start with flirtatious behavior throughout the day. The little pinches on the backside. The little kisses on the neck. Those are some of the little things that keep your woman going and emotionally charged. Sending her the daily, "I love you" email first thing when you get to work makes a difference. Sending the random affectionate text messages do the same trick.

I've had several women tell me that it wasn't about the big things they had received from their men; it was the accumulation of the smaller things that mattered. In baseball terms, you want to be the player with the higher more consistent batting average. Always looking for the homerun will dramatically lower your batting average. The manager would rather keep the sure thing and not the hit or miss guy. Again, the accumulation of smaller things ensures longevity.

That's something to think about if you are the man that shows up only on occasions and are missing in action any other time. Showing little bits of appreciation for your woman on a consistent basis will also alleviate the strain of trying to produce a massive act of appreciation on a designated day. I can honestly say that the majority of women would rather have it consistently than only on holidays, birthdays and anniversaries. If you don't believe me, just ask your woman or conduct your own survey. If I've said it one or a thousand times in my lifetime, if you show your woman that you truly appreciate her, she'll literally go to war for you.

A good woman knows when a man is trying to appreciate them. I know that as a man, it could be a bit puzzling just thinking of ways of showing appreciation, let alone think of something unique and creative to do. A good woman will appreciate the effort alone. It may just be a homemade card, she'll appreciate it. Even if you surprise he with God knows what for dinner, she will grin and bear it out of appreciation.

So, certainly, you see appreciation is not all about the material things. Just the efforts or actions put into it could be more than enough. The main thing out of it all is making an attempt. Any woman can tell you that. It's nothing like making an attempt and although it may be a bust, your woman looking you square in your eyes and telling you, "Baby, it's okay." "At least you tried and that's all that matters." She can see the disappointment in your eyes but she's more thrilled about the fact that you were delighted enough in her to even try.

I can almost count on it that she will be on the phone with her friends boasting about what you did. She may not even mention how it turned out but her friends will be envious. I don't know what it is, but women have a knack for making a story more invigorating than it really was. Thank God for our good women huh? Love your woman, appreciate your woman and she will be by your side forever. It's all about the effort!

## *Choosing Your Battles Wisely*

*Sanballat and Geshem sent me this message: "Come, let us meet together in one of the villages on the plain of Ono." But they were scheming to harm me; so I sent messengers to them with this reply: "I am carrying on a great project and cannot go down. Why should the work stop while I leave it and go down to you?"*

**Nehemiah 6:2-3**

The previously stated scriptures reference the vision that Nehemiah had to rebuild the walls of Jerusalem. When dealing with your personal vision, you are bound to come across several opposing forces. It's only a sign of you doing right or going in the right direction. It's how you react to your opposition that determines how far you will go with your vision.

The definition of a battle can be defined as *a conflict between two opposing groups or individuals.* In order to have a battle, one of the two, if not both, is in disagreement with one another. With the several types of people and personalities in the world, you are bound to have a disagreement with someone about something.

It's inevitable. The key to success is not to get involved in every battle that presents itself before you. You must pick and choose your battles wisely. Every battle does not have your name on it.

> **"The key to success is not get involved in every battle that presents itself before you."**

One thing for sure, battles take time. If you are spending all of your time engaged in battle, how do you have time to do anything productive in your life? You can't. Your mind is constantly stuck in battle mode. When your mind is stuck in battle mode, you walk around on edge. Your people skills dwindle to a minimum because you are constantly thinking that everyone is out to engage in battle with you or the opposite, you're looking to engage in battle with someone else.

Let me tell you, not all people that you run across are out to get you. Don't go barking up the wrong tree. If you took the time to realize this, you would probably see that God could put someone in your path to assist you in life, but you would have to see it first. That person could be in a noticeable place but if you have a closed mind, you would overlook them. This starts with the changing of your mind. *Do not conform any longer to the pattern of this world, but be transformed by the renewing of your mind. Then you will be able to test and approve what God's will is--his good, pleasing and perfect will.* **Romans 12:2**

## "If you are spending all of your time engaged in battle, how do you have time to do anything productive in your life?"

I know that you may have been burned in the past or even been embarrassed in the past but that does not mean that all people are that way. Come out of your shell and live a little. You will need to understand that the devil stays busy and there is always going to be someone that is going to test you or try you. Even Jesus himself got tested when he was led by the Spirit into the desert. **Matthew 4:1**

There are going to be people that do certain things simply out of spite to see where your mind is. How many of you have had the experience as a young boy in which you had to deal with teasing in school? How did you react? At that time, the teasing may have appeared to be a horrendous act against you. What you maybe didn't realize is the source of the teasing against you was jealousy. Don't let another person's mental dysfunction get to you. You can't engage in everything. If someone doesn't like you so what?

Brush it off. Be steadfast in your mental process and stay focused.

## "The devil stays busy and there is always going to be someone that is going to test you or try you."

There's always going to be people that will have something to say about what you are doing or where you are going. I believe they are called, "haters." *"Blessed are you when people insult you, persecute you and falsely say all kinds of evil against you because of me."* **Matthew 5:11** Some people are just bitter and hateful. You must recognize it, accept it, and keep it moving. I heard this one time and it's so true. Picture yourself as a boat. A boat floats on top of water just fine. When does a boat sink? A boat sinks when it allows what's on the outside to get into the inside of it.

What's on the outside of the boat represents the challenges before you from other people. Don't let those challenges inside of your boat for they will surely sink you. The speaker closed by stating, "You must ride on top of the waves of life." The sooner you realize that some people just love wallowing in their own misery you will be golden.

If you are trying to go somewhere in life, you don't have time to waste by entertaining all of the riff raff that comes before you. Most of the times, it's just a ploy to distract you or slow you down. If your mind is right, you will be able to see through it all. Now, I'm not saying to never engage into battle but rather get your mind right and choose it wisely. There are some things out there that are battle worthy.

If you have children and someone comes against your children, that's a battle worthy encounter. If someone comes against your house, that's a battle worthy encounter. You have to decide which ones are worthy and which ones are not. You can't be a hot headed man trying to battle everything. That will be a total waste of time. Think about how many encounters cross you on a daily basis. If you engage in all of them, how much time do you leave yourself for doing something productive? Hardly any time at all.

Let's try this from another angle. Think about it with me. A battle exerts a bit of energy. That's mental energy and emotional energy. It's not just physical energy. It's like when you go to the gym to work out. So much energy has been excerpted that your body requires time to recoup. That's why doctors suggest that you workout every other day and not every day. You're giving your muscles time to recoup. That way they're able to respond and function properly. With all of that being said let's remove the physical aspect of it all. Let's throw the gym out of the equation also. Let's bring your mind and emotions into the equation using the same logic. Your mind and your emotions require recoup time as well. Remember, engaging in every confrontation in your everyday life exerts mental and emotional energy not just physical.

Now that I have gotten your mind on the proper path, let's divert this to one's self. Let's do a bit of self-checking. Have you ever stopped to think that the reason you walk around with a hot temper all day is because you never gave your mind and emotions time to recoup? The more you engage in confrontation, the hotter your temper will become. It's just like a muscle. The more you work it, the stronger it will become. It may not be them! It may be you! You're the one building the mental and emotional muscles!

You walk around hot tempered stating they are on your nerves or pissing you off all along strengthening these muscles. That's the problem. Too many people want to cast the blame on someone else instead of facing themselves in the mirror. You're so big and bad when it comes to dealing with other people. Why are you just walking past the mirror instead of stopping to take a look? Are you afraid of what you may see? Are you afraid to look at the person with the same destructive behavior that you so call despise? What gives you the right to even part your lips? You should check YOURSELF instead of checking the next man or woman! Do a bit of self-exploration every once and a while.

In closing, sticking to my message to choose battles wisely, try starting with the battle you have going on within. Until you fix yourself, your temper won't get better. The people around you won't get better. The world won't get better either. It won't get better until people like you stand in front of the mirror and take responsibility for their own behavior and actions. When you break down Earth to a smaller scope it represents a collection of many people.

Let's take it an even smaller scope. Let's go from the Earth to countries and then to states. Let's go from states to counties. Let's go from counties to cities and then to neighborhoods. Now go from neighborhoods to our homes and each individual in a home. Take that individual which would be you and correct your destructive DNA by self-exploration. When you correct YOUR destructive DNA it will affect the people around you in a positive way. A new found corrected DNA and personality will spread like wild fire. Now take the smallest scope which is YOU and reverse the path that I have taken to come down to YOU. YOU, correcting yourself will correct your home. A corrected home corrects the neighborhood. A corrected neighborhood corrects a city. A corrected city corrects the county. A corrected county corrects the state. A corrected state corrects the country. A corrected country corrects the WHOLE PLANET! Look in the mirror!

## *Celebrating Yourself*

Although you are the foundation of the home, sometimes you may not get the appreciation that you truly deserve. True, the foundation is the most important part of the home but it is also the part of the home that is not visible. With that being said, you must find a way to celebrate yourself. You're the least recognized although you hold great importance. A celebration is defined as *a joyful occasion to mark a happy event.* Have you ever held a celebration for yourself? Better yet, do you truly know how to celebrate yourself?

It's unfortunate but as a man you could receive little if any acknowledgement for your daily efforts. The taking out the trash, fixing the cars, putting food on the table, protecting the house, and paying the bills, do not warrant a huge acknowledgement in most households. Sometimes as a man, you could feel a bit underappreciated. I know you're a man and you're taught to make sure your home is in order but you deserve a bit of recognition also. Every time you turn around you see acts of celebration that are geared towards the woman. If her birthday isn't enough, you have Valentine's Day, Christmas, and possibly Mother's Day.

As a man, you go out of your way to ensure these days are special for your woman. Most of the time holiday or not we go out of our way to ensure our woman is happy in order to have a peaceful home. What holidays do you have? You have your birthday and Father's day, if you have a child or children. When your day comes, how many times have you set yourself up by thinking you would get rewarded to the same degree you have shown others in your home year round? I'm not saying all men are treated this way. I'm just suggesting that what you receive on that one day may not equate to what you put into your household on an annual basis.

> **"The taking out the trash, fixing the cars, putting food on the table, protecting the house, and paying the bills do not warrant a huge acknowledgement."**

No, this isn't an act of selfishness. This is more of a wakeup call for you. Do YOU for once. Do what makes you genuinely happy. Better yet, have you taken the time to figure out what makes you genuinely happy? Where I'm trying to go with this should be simple but believe it or not, there are several of you that don't know how to celebrate yourselves. You invest so much time in pleasing others that you feel like a fish out of water when it comes to celebrating yourself. The time that you finally have to yourself, you end up not doing anything because you don't receive the opportunity often enough to know what to do.

### "Have you taken the time to figure out what makes you genuinely happy?"

Women celebrate themselves all of the time by going to the spa or going shopping. Why can't you as a hard-working man do it also? After all of the hustle and bustle in the house, you need time to yourself to take care of just YOU. This is that moment when you think about you and no one else. Most men only need a few simple things for satisfaction as it is. This includes peace, quiet, and possible harmony. The problem with this is most men don't get this in their homes. Mainly, if you have a spouse or kids, throw all of those previously mentioned simple things out of the window. It isn't happening, unless you have a man cave out back.

Celebration time for you is very essential. Please excuse the over exaggeration but I truly believe the lack of celebration by men can also play a huge part in their lifespans. Getting away from it all and getting away from hearing "baby" every five minutes is like Heaven on Earth for man. You get to press the reset button and take the opportunity to rejuvenate yourself. Without celebrating yourself there may be a smile on the outside but there is little or no joy on the inside. Although you may be afraid to admit it in front of your spouse, can you attest to that a little piece of you that died when you became engaged in a relationship or marriage?

I ask you, if you had no one to answer to or no one to care about, what would you be doing that makes you fulfilled and happy? The answer to that question is what you need to set aside time for in order to celebrate yourself. I'm not saying go overboard but find the things that make you happy. Whether it's going fishing, going shopping for a new suit and tie, going out shooting pool, or even taking a road trip with the fellas, find something to celebrate you with and do it.

I challenge every man to celebrate themselves at least once a month or once a week if you could. Get away from it all for a while. You will be amazed at how your energy level will suddenly increase. Your hunger to live life and not let life dictate you will increase. This will also translate to loving your spouse at a higher level due to a new found happiness within. Being refreshed and not bogged down by all of the worries in life can act as an aphrodisiac for you. Having a clear head can increase your energy level which in turn, can allow you to focus your newfound energy towards your spouse.

> **"If you had no one to answer to or no one to care about, what would you be doing that makes you fulfilled and happy?"**

To the woman reader, "Allowing your man the time to celebrate himself will ultimately strengthen your relationship." His love for you will increase emotionally and intimately. Just the fact that you have allowed him to break away from it all for a moment of time is an attraction to him. You are basically saying to him that you trust him and that you for once understand the burdens that he goes through on a daily basis.

You are also showing him that you can act unselfishly by allotting him this time as well. He spends so much time catering to you, while secretly envying you. This is due to him not being allotted the same personal celebration time that he allows you to have. I speak for the men, "Give him time to celebrate and he'll meet you later for the after party." Celebrate yourselves!

## *Help! I Need My Altar!*

An altar can be seen as a place where you would go by yourself to get away from everything. It's that secret and quiet place where you go to speak with your Heavenly Father. It's the place where you go to get those heavy burdens off of your heart. You know what I mean. Those things that no one else could dare know about. It's the place where you have total peace, which allows you to lay it all out on the table, leaving nothing behind. So, before I go any further, I must ask. Do you have such a place? Do you have an altar?

Life can come at you from several different angles which could seriously cause pressure buildup. You are constantly feeling the pressures of this and that on a daily basis. Just being the head of your house brings added responsibilities and pressure. Just as God made Adam responsible for everything in the Garden of Eden, you are responsible for everything under your covering, which includes your house. You have the responsibility of knowing that whatever condition your house is in, primarily comes down to you. I understand there may be potholes along the way so no, I'm not saying because you aren't monetarily sound that you are a failure. What I AM saying is that you have to hold down your house. You have to be the foundation!

## "Do you have an altar?"

I focus on being the foundation not because it's the divine order of the household but to illustrate the pressures that men have in keeping their homes together. Man is simply man. That means we are not some immortal Gods, but simply men. We have our weaknesses. The beatings of everyday life can simply wear you down not only physically but mentally. I remember seeing the advertisement a few years back for the product Calgon. Calgon was a bathing product marketed towards those that were stressed out from everyday life. The marketing phrase was, "Calgon take me away." Though the commercial may have been targeted mostly towards women, it brought something to mind.

You often see products that are marketed towards women to ease the tensions of everyday life but what about the men? I know often times you are too macho to admit that you are beat physically and mentally, but deep down inside you yearn for that escape. You yearn for that special place where you could go to escape and be at one. Be at total peace.

Again, do you have such a place? How do you cope when you've had a hard day at the job? How do you escape the feeling of not having a moment to yourself because you have been bum rushed from the kids or the wife from the time you walked into the door? How do you escape when the bills are surmounting and you have the slightest clue of how they will get paid? It's not always monetary. Maybe you've done something that you are completely ashamed of or you have a deep dark secret that you must confess.

Let's be real for a moment. Yes, it may be secret to someone else but we all know God knows everything that you're going through. Since HE knows already, why hide it? It's like Adam when he ate from the tree of good and evil. God already knew what had taken place which is why he showed up at the Garden of Eden asking for an explanation. Out of pure foolishness, we see Adam thinking he could hide from God. God is not going to kill you. HE is our father. What father do you know that would kill his child? So why run and hide? Instead, you see a caring father that simply wants to have a relationship with his child. A caring father that wants to teach and mold his child into becoming the best he could be.

**"God is not going to kill you. HE is our father."**

I have to use myself for example. As a man, there has been some things in my life that had me literally about to lose my mind. Through experiences in my life I had to realize something though. It's nothing like the experience of developing a relationship with my Heavenly Father. I say "currently" simply because I will be in a continuous relationship with my Father till the day I die. The relationship even continues to Heaven. Believe me when I say Earthly role models are wonderful. They can provide you with an Earthly wealth of knowledge but they too must answer to someone. That someone is God.

It's like a chain of command and it all points to God as the leader. Earthly role models are there for immediate knowledge while God's wisdom is eternal. That simply means that God's knowledge will last throughout your lifetime. I will admit. I had a huge struggle in the premature stages of my relationship with God. I had issues with talking and worshipping someone that wasn't even there to see. You're on the stoop or in the shower seemingly talking to yourself. If someone were to see me they would surely think I was crazy but I continued to do it because I could sense a presence was there. I kept utilizing every bit of quiet time that I had in the mornings to talk to God. I still do it to this day.

I look back at my life today. I have made some decisions that were a bit dense. My issue that I had to face at that moment in time was a result of me not going to my secret place where God and I could talk about it first. I didn't wait on anyone or anything, I just did it. Does this sound familiar to any of you? Guess who I ran back to after it fell through the cracks? I was right there front and center in my secret place requesting God's presence. The problem many of us have is that we see God as our clean up man. We react out of our flesh and when we see that we had acted out of foolishness, we resort back to Him. You must do better and seek knowledge from God before reacting.

Your altar is that open channel for eternal knowledge. You should be hungry to receive knowledge obtained at your sacred meeting place. Using myself as an example, there were numerous occasions where I had something weighing heavily on my mind. I would go out to the stoop with an immediate train of thought, immediate meaning what I felt or saw at that given moment. I was only thinking about what my eyes and mind could fathom at that time, almost as if I were a bit depleted in the faith category. Boy was I enlightened. All of those days sitting outside of my home focusing on an immediate situation were slowly turning things around for me. Things started being revealed to me.

At first, I would get a glimpse but didn't fully understand. I would come back the next day and I would see a little more. This cycle kept repeating itself and the more I asked, the more he revealed. The more I asked for clarity, the more defined it started to become. Through strengthening my relationship with God in my sacred place I came away with a plan for my life. I now had direction. All of the delays before were all pieces of the plan He had for me. So, your altar can bring revelation to you, as I present to you, "The Facets of Man."

You must understand that we serve a very systematic God. Meeting God at your altar provides that open channel between God and yourself where He can reveal your next move. If you've ever played chess you know what I mean. You plot your move in your head first before you actually make the move. Meeting God at the altar provides the direction in which your next move should be made. Although you may not see it, it will be revealed to you. You just need to have faith in the instructions coming from your manufacturer. Each move will be a calculated move for His purpose and timing, not yours. All you can do at that moment is praise His name. You must recognize WHO gave you what you have today. It wasn't you, it was Him.

There are doors that have opened up for you that you had no idea would open but they did. Your eyes have not seen the glory that will be bestowed upon you. Don't go by what you see right now because it will frustrate you every time. I've heard before, sight is the enemy of vision. The devil will trick you into believing what you currently see and not where you are going. You must believe in where you are going. Again, you obtain this knowledge in your sacred place.

> **"The devil will trick you into believing what you currently see and not where you are going."**

What this all boils down to is getting to know your Heavenly Father on a more personal level. How do you accomplish this you ask? You form this intimate bond with Him by creating an altar for yourself. He knows the burdens you hold deep down inside. He just wants you to open up that channel of communication with Him so that the both of you can have a relationship with one another. He wants to love you and mold you into what He has designed for you to be. You were born with an already pre-destined purpose. You were just born to start it. Stop running from it. The longer you run from it, the more you waste time to be what you were designed to be.

Every time you approach your altar He provides you with bits and pieces as to what your life is to become as long as you continue to confide in Him. I know it may seem rough in your current situation but God is just placing you right where He wants you to be. Each step along the way, whether good or bad is just adding another facet to you, making you more and more valuable. Seek God before you make a move. Allow Him to be the lantern in your darkness. So I close by asking, "Where is your altar?" "Do you have such a place?"

## *Come On! Where's Your Pride?*

    Pride, the very word alone makes the average man's chest stick out. I mean really, who can tell you anything right? Though it may not be to that extreme, it's almost certain that a male will wear his pride on his shoulders at some point in time. You're the head of your house right? If not too careful, that title alone could find you being overly prideful. By all means, don't get me wrong, it's very well okay to have pride. I wouldn't see it any other way, but the key is to not let your pride affect your outlook on the world.

Walking around with your pride on your shoulders suggests that you may not have any errant ways yourself and we know you do. We all do unless we became God himself overnight. What causes a man to wear his pride on his shoulders? Let's delve into this a bit. Could it be the fact that we are naturally dominant beings? We internally have a natural instinct derived from the first man on Earth by the name of Adam whom God created first. Being first, means that you are responsible for everything and anything that comes afterwards. That very derivative instinct could cause you to walk around with your chest stuck out because you feel there is nothing before you. It triggers the, "You can't tell me anything" attitude.

**"Walking around with your pride on your shoulders suggests that you may not have any errant ways yourself and we know you do."**

Ever have your spouse attempt to tell you something and right or wrong, you're not trying to hear it? Besides, who is SHE to tell you anything right? She was not derived from Adam. You were! What happens a lot of times? Yeah, you've guessed it. You're left looking foolish and once your pride kicks in, you rarely want to admit to her that you were wrong. I must use which is probably the two most common examples when it comes to us and our female counterparts.

The first example would be driving around town trying to find your location. She originally suggested that you map it out online. You boasted that you knew exactly where you were going. After several drives around the block, your mind tells you internally that you're lost but you dare not let her know. As soon as she suggests that perhaps the both of you may be lost, you're quick to get on the defensive with her even though yes, you WERE wrong and lost. Your pride just wouldn't let you admit to her that you may be wrong.

The second example I would like to give is confrontation. How many times has your macho behavior gotten you into even bigger trouble then had you just walked away? Say for instance you and your spouse somehow ended up in a confrontation with someone else. Your spouse was quick to dismiss the meaningless behavior but you were not having that. You must take action! Besides, you're not a soft man are you? You have to prove that your hours of training in the gym were not void.

You blacked out and you proceeded to pummeling the other person who started the confrontation not realizing that there were people around watching and they've already alerted the police. Yes, you may have won the fight, victory for you! Those handcuffs just tend to make it hard to raise your hands like Rocky don't they? What did you prove? You have a bloody face and now you are spending money you could have spent elsewhere getting bailed out of jail. You think pride had something to do with it? Don't worry about it we both know the answer, though your pride may not let you admit it.

This brings me back to our female counterparts. How many good women have you let walk out of the door because of your pride? Yeah, the one that got away. She wanted something more, yet your pride would not allow for you to compromise. How many of you regret that one to this day? She has gone on with her life, found a man that was not too prideful to compromise a few things, and now they are happily married with kids. You with your prideful self, has to be reminded of it constantly because you all go to the same church and you see them every Sunday.

The point I'm trying to make is at what point does the light bulb click on? When will you realize that being overly prideful will make you look like a fool? *Pride goes before destruction, a haughty spirit before a fall.* **Proverbs 16:18**. God hates a prideful person. He will bring down your self-made walls of pride and leave you exposed to deal with the world alone. Let's be honest, a lot of times you walk around being prideful is to mask the insecurities that you are dealing with on the inside anyway. You internally know that you have a deficiency in one area so you create this false persona to cover it up. You can't tell me that you are made perfectly by God because you are not! If you were, what need is there for God?

You walk around with your futile chest out and your nose up in the clouds as if the world is beneath you. You are nothing! Humble yourselves before God before He humbles you! How do you think you got the talent that may have provided you with lifestyle that you live today? How do you think your limbs are still functioning properly in order to move around from day to day? God allowed for those things to happen!

That job that you covet so much could be snatched away from you in a blink of an eye! Think it won't? What is the state of our economy today? Jobs are not as plentiful as they used to be. Companies are chomping at the bit to reduce headcount in order to reduce costs. Be warned! You may walk around thinking just because you may have been blessed with the physical attributes to be a standout athlete that God can't reach you? Boom! The news reporter reads, "Star athlete was involved in a life threatening car accident and he is now in critical condition." Humble yourselves! You walk around thinking you are a ladies man because you have plenty of sleep partners and the doctor tells you that you now have AIDS. Be warned!

Your pride may have made you feel as though you had it all and there was nothing better than you. You ever notice how the harder you worked on a self-made idea, the more it became stunted? Ever feel as though you were going in circles with something? Like you were a hamster on the wheel? You tried harder but you were making no progress? Maybe you were becoming too prideful. The more prideful you were becoming, the more God was afflicting you. The Lord was shutting down your self-made ideas to break you down. Until you acknowledged Him you were not making any progress.

I must tell you. You could work yourself to the bone until you are 65 years old and still never get where you wanted to be in life. You could walk around thinking you are this and that, yet you're 45 and alone. You could walk around not entertaining the angels of God that come before you on the side of the roads because you are too good and wonder why you have never been blessed. You could find yourself at church being too prideful to worship and tithe but wonder why you've just been diagnosed with a serious medical condition. Humble yourselves! Remove the self-made pride because if you don't, God will!

## *Humility*

Humility is something we all can take heed to. In actuality, it's something we all should practice more often. For those of you that may not be familiar with the word humility, it is the act of being humble. Showing humility is one of the hardest things to do in the world we live in today because it can be seen as a sign of weakness. We live in the day and age where everyone is trying to get the jump on the next person and showing humility won't work right? Wrong! That's the issue we have today. If we all had a broader understanding of the word and had a better understanding of the act, the world wouldn't be in the shape it's in today.

Let me provide a very common scenario that the majority of the working class may face on a daily basis. How many times have you been in traffic and wanted to change lanes? What happens a lot of times? As soon as you put on your signal, the car in the lane you want to switch to speeds up not allowing you to pass. Was it really that serious? If only the other driver would have just let you switch lanes, everything would have gone with the flow. Instead, they felt as though they needed to make it a competition as if it were a big game or something. Happen to you often? How funny is it that no, you're not chasing them down shooting the "bird" but you end up passing them in traffic a bit further down the highway. They have now become a victim of the same situation? Exactly my point! Where did the lack of humility get other person? One meaning of humility in the Bible is one of loving others, which does not translate to you being a wimp!

## "Do nothing out of selfish ambition or vain conceit, but in humility consider others better than you."

### Philippians 2:3

In this chapter, I'm going to entice you to dig deeper within in an attempt to find yourself in humility. Look at the verse above. It states to do nothing out of selfish ambition or vain conceit. Ask yourself, "How often do I take the selfishness out of acts that I perform for others?" "Do I have an internal motive for what I'm doing?" The rest of the verse says to consider others better than you. I would be telling a tall tale if I didn't admit that it takes a strong individual to put others before you. It takes an act of selflessness no doubt. This rings truth in a household.

How many of you are in a relationship? How many times have you had a desire but you put it on hold or modified your desire to satisfy your spouse or the children? You could have had a desire for the latest model sports car but you settled for the four door sedan or minivan. You could have had an awesome desire of your very own man cave plastered with your favorite sports team but that room is now converted into a child's room or an office. You could have been saving your money for the latest high definition television but Valentine's Day came around.

Those are just a few instances but I must ask you, "Although it may have taken you a remarkable amount of strength to perform these acts, did it make you appear weak?" I'll answer it for you. No, it didn't. You were simply putting others before you. I do have to point out how God works though. How many of you have put others before you regarding something you may have wanted and then turned around in the near future getting blessed with what you wanted or something even better?

You've gone the whole year putting your spouse and kids before you. On Christmas you found yourself walking into the family room to see your high definition television with a bow on it just for you? Maybe when you're finally able to afford that sports car, the price you were quoted initially, had miraculously dropped. That's God at his finest.

### "A gentle answer turns away wrath, but a harsh word stirs up anger" Proverbs 15:1

Let's touch on displaying the act of humility during confrontation. Having humility in a confrontation requires you to first, be comfortable in God and secondly, be comfortable in yourself. Let me reference the scripture above. A gentle answer turns away wrath. How many times have you been approached by someone who's out to argue with you no matter what? They may have had a bad day so they're dead set on taking it out on someone. This could be at work or even in the bedroom with your spouse after a long day's work. Let me use the latter for example. You're kicking back in the bed getting ready to watch the ball game in total peace. Your spouse walks in from work in a rampage. Now, this has nothing to do with you, but you're caught in the crossfire.

Your mind is jacked up for the game, not for her intentionally started quarrel. It could be something as minor as letting the kids have ice cream before dinner. We know ice cream before dinner is not a life or death situation but it was something for them to use as an open door to get out their pinned up frustration. If you haven't figured it out by now as you jump up from your ever so comfortable surroundings, that the ice cream is not the root of the problem. They know that and you quickly realize it as well.

So, as they charge in a rampage to meet you face to face, you politely let them know that the ice cream will not kill them. It is no big deal. You bring that to their attention as you focus back on the game. As disruptive as that could be, it also could be a bit humorous inside to see their blank expression. Your spouse came in thinking you would engage in warfare and you simply raised the white flag and dismissed it all upfront. As they sit there a bit perplexed, you've turned away wrath.

Let's address the second part of the scripture. A harsh word stirs up anger. Let's rewind to the moment your spouse walked into the room in a rampage. Instead of providing a gentle answer, you provided harsh words since after all, they did, interrupt your peace. A simple gesture of giving the kids ice cream before dinner has turned into a full blown argument. Why, you ask? Simply because you provided harsh words and opened up the door for their pinned in frustrations. Now, it doesn't have anything to do with the ice cream because it has gone to another level. In these types of situations what normally happens is you end up missing your highly anticipated game.

The both of you end up going on and on over something that didn't originate at home. It originated outside of your home. You ever hear of dropping whatever you have on your shoulders at the door and forgetting about it? If not, that's a great practice to take on in your home. Although it may be a rough task, practice getting yourself together and leaving it all at the door before entering your home. After time it will become normality and you have minimized the chances of chaos from the outside creeping into your home. All of this should be done in an attempt of humility.

**"Get rid of all bitterness, rage and anger, brawling and slander, along with every form of malice. Be kind and compassionate to one another, forgiving each other, just as in Christ God forgave you" Ephesians 4:31-32**

I would like to quickly touch on those who like to pump themselves up. Once you understand the true meaning of humility, you don't have to over exert yourself. You need to be comfortable in yourself and your own abilities excluding the braggadocios behavior. Remove the facade. We've all heard of the phrase, "You don't have to lie to kick it." That's a colloquialism meaning you don't have to lie about what you have and who you are.

In closing, if you don't already, try practicing putting others before you. Jesus Himself displayed the act of humility by washing feet. Read John 13:12. If Jesus could do it, KNOWING that He didn't have to, I know YOU can. I would like for you to resort back to this chapter a few weeks from now or it may be a few days and think about how you were truly blessed from this change in perspective. Again, being humble does not mean weakness. Being humble shows signs of inner strength, confidence, composure, intelligence, and faithfulness. Being selfish and spiteful will get you nowhere.

I know at times you may have the exact words that could shut a person down but it's not all about that. That's not displaying humility. Remember what a gentle answer would do. Get in the habit of being humble. Get in the habit of doing for others. When you put others before you, you will be amazed at how things begin to flow for you. Just like the traffic scenario, making it a pointless competition just brings frustration when all along, the transition could have allowed for everything to flow smoothly. Work on being sensitive to other's needs. It's not all about you. Could you imagine how the world would be if we all practiced some form of humility? Imagine how enjoyable the world would be and how much easier your life would be. Remember when you were younger? What did they teach you?

***"Treat others as you would like to be treated."***

# Part II

# What's Your Motivation?

## Give Me A Plan

***"The LORD Almighty has sworn, "Surely, as I have planned, so it will be, and as I have purposed, so it will stand." Isaiah 14:24"***

    The majority of you were taught at a young age that you were to be the providers of your home. These teachings were drilled to you as an adolescent so by the time you grew older; you were already programmed to be in provider mode. Whether it was providing for yourself or your family, you knew you had to do what it took to survive. You may have been faced with a few questions. How would I provide? Where would I start on the road to becoming a provider? Who could I turn to for guidance to show me how to be a great provider? Junior needs a new pair of shoes for school. My wife needs a new car. My daughter needs a new cheerleading uniform. How will I afford these things? Life is currently dealing me a bad deck. How could I turn this thing around? I'm trying to provide by doing this but it doesn't seem to be working. What am I doing wrong?

Has any of these worries or questions ever come up in your life? I could sit here and tell you that I haven't been in the same boat myself. I could sit here and act as if everything in my life was perfect and I've never had to deal with such things, but that would be a lie. I too had fallen into this category and still do at times. When my financial situation was not up to par during a period in my life, I felt a bit unsuccessful as a man. I could sit here and tell you that I would immediately go to a private area and have a one on one with God.

No, this didn't always happen this way and it wasn't that easy to do. I would become instantly frustrated when I had no money. I allowed my financial failures to control my moods and even my thought process. I allowed my finances to define my success as a man and a provider. It got to the point that I thought about taking what I knew wasn't mine so that I could have money in my pockets. If I didn't have it, I was going to get it by any means necessary.

I'm ashamed to say that I coveted money more than I coveted my relationship with God at one point in time. I knew where I wanted to be financially but at the time I wasn't there. I wasn't even close. The lint in my pockets presented proof of that fact. I would ask, "What am I doing wrong?" I would say to myself, "I have all of the ambition in the world but I'm not getting anywhere." The underlining issue was that I didn't know where I was going in life. I was clueless. I had no a plan for anything in which several of us don't. How can you get somewhere and you don't know how you're going to get there? You need some sense of direction mapped out for yourself. Where are you walking if you have no road in front of you? That's where a plan comes into play. You must have a plan in order to reach those vivid images you keep seeing in your head. You can't just say you want it and it just magically appears. You must have a plan.

It wasn't until I started strengthening my relationship with God that a plan was revealed for my life. It got to the point that instead of going into this huge tantrum, I had to talk to God about my situations. Mankind was not helping me at all. I later realized that God was causing me to have these financial failures in my life to bring me closer to Him. It's funny how things happen. The things you covet most will be removed all in His plan to steer you back to Him. Stop focusing on the material aspect so much. Start focusing on the spiritual aspect. Your plan is going to originally come from God anyway, so you might as well stop what you're currently doing and seek him for it.

When these things begin to be revealed to you, never lose sight of who gave it to you. Remember, your plan materialized from God in the first place. It's just now; He's providing you with the steps to get there. I know the natural reaction when making progress is to get excited. It's human nature. That's okay and great because it will motivate you to keep going but you must fight off the temptation of thinking YOU did it and not God. Always remember that it came from God and stay humble. Allow God to order your steps. You must be diligent by staying in God's word and have a sensitive ear to what He is trying to tell you. In due time, bits and pieces will be revealed to you, relating to the masterful plan for your life.

> ***"For I know the plans I have for you," declares the LORD, "plans to prosper you and not to harm you, plans to give you hope and a future.* Jeremiah 29:11"**

That's why you should make absolutely sure your plan is of Him and not all your own. It's tricky because you must differentiate between what part of the plan is from God and what part is your own. You must weed out anything that could possibly be out of your selfish ways. I say this because, if your plan is not from God, there's a great chance your plan will not prosper as much as you had intended it to. Therefore, you may want to ease off a bit and let God do the driving. It's no doubt that God is a better strategist than you are.

Take heed to what I am about to say next. A plan from God will require heavy faith. Why you ask? As soon as you start living out the plan that God has for you, there will be distractions that try to derail you and the plan! You must stay focused on God through it all. Let's use the example of Peter walking on water. As long as Peter kept his eyes fixed on Jesus, he could walk on water, but as soon as he got distracted and looked away, he began to sink. You must not allow for yourself to sink because of distractions. It never fails, as soon as you start doing well and going into the right direction, something or someone comes to distract you? Like they say, "Bigger levels bring bigger devils." You must be prepared and you must view it all with the proper perspective.

Distractions mean success is on its way. Just don't become influenced or tempted by them. I speak from my own personal experience. Distractions alone are what caused me to write this book now instead of a young boy fresh out of high school. Though they didn't delete the vivid images I say, they did delay them. Thank God for not giving up on me while I fought through the distractions.

> **"Distractions mean success is on its way if you don't become influenced by them."**

I do want to set the record straight when it comes to distractions. There are several that confuse distractions with life. Life and distractions are two separate things though I've heard several people say, "Life happened." Life didn't happen, distractions did. Life is a period of time. It's the period of time you have from birth to death. A distraction is a state of mental confusion at that point in time. Get it? It's a state of confusion at a point in time. After that point in time, you still have time for correction.

 Life didn't stop you from achieving your goals in life. All life did was allow for you to live another day. Life just provided you with another shot at making better choices and coming back to the plan laid out for you. Another 24 hours. So the term, "life happened" should never come out of your mouth again. Life is just the span of time you have to figure it all out. So, actually, distractions happened, not life! You can't keep allowing for yourself to become distracted and burn another 24 hours of your life. Do you honestly think you will live forever? Take control of your life and say to heck with the distractions! Make up your mind from this point forth that you will maximize every 24 hours of your life God has blessed you with, because tomorrow is not promised to you.

Now that you know distractions are headed your way, you should be able to recognize them when they appear. Knowing is half the battle. If you didn't know they would be coming, you wouldn't be able to plan ahead. Planning ahead allows for you to stick to the plan while giving distractions the stiff arm as a running back would a linebacker. It's all about the plan. So I ask you, "Do you have a plan for you and your family?" If so, is it a plan from you or God? Who do you listen to before your next step? Where do your steps get you? Are you better off afterwards or back to the drawing board trying to devise another route?

For those of you that are still in search of a plan, the next segment is for you. First of all, don't be discouraged. God works on his own timetable. So, when He gets ready to bless you with the plan for your life, your blessing will come. Know that this will not go off of your timetable but His. It will take patience and faith but it will be worth the wait. I know I found myself trying to change up my prayer, thinking that it would speed things up but it didn't happen. I'm into my 30's now and I've been asking for a plan since my teen years. God is just now revealing to me what my gifts are, along with the plan for my life. It shall come to pass. Stay sensitive to those things God is trying to show you. Take note of them, as they are little golden nuggets of wisdom, revealing to you your plan piece by piece.

As I conclude, I say to you, "Men need God given visions and God given plans to follow." You need a plan. Your family needs you to have a plan. Without it, there will be no sense of direction for you or your home. *"Where there is no vision, the people perish."* **Proverbs 29:18**

Where there is no vision the people will do what? Perish! We are the leaders of our homes. If YOU, being the head, don't have a God given vision and God given plan, what do you think happens to your house? YOU provide the vision for your home because if you don't, your home could get direction from something or someone else. You can obtain it if you have the right plan to get there.

## *Submitted To The Plan*

    I wanted to take the moment to briefly discuss a topic that rarely comes up when it comes to your God given plan. Though it may not be very popular, it still holds great importance. It's the act of submission. When God gives you a plan for your life, you must submit to it. It doesn't matter what the plan may be, you must submit. Let's go back in time when you had no Godly direction for your life. Everything you tried derailed because it was not part of the plan God had for you. It was your plan alone.

After nothing worked, you found yourself on your knees begging God to bless you with a plan for your life. Then He revealed it to you. How did you take it? Was the end result what you envisioned for yourself? Did you say to yourself, "I can't see myself doing that?" "I'm not ready yet." This is what I heard one pastor state as a "choking moment." He referred to it as a "choking moment" because at that very moment, God told you to do something, yet you choked. You froze up. It doesn't matter how you phrase it, you didn't submit to it.

What caused you to not submit to the plan God gave you? He gave it to you so it MUST be good for you, yet you fled from it. Could it be you were not ready for what He showed you? Could it be what you were shown would cause you to become corrected? How many times have you heard of someone running from their calling? Now that you have been shown a plan from God, is that someone you? People run from their callings because they don't want to submit to what God has shown them. Too many times we are rebellious to what we KNOW we should be doing. What are you afraid of?

I could tell you what several of you may be afraid of. Several of you are afraid because of who the plan materialized from. The very thought of having to correct yourselves because it came from God has caused a bit of hesitancy to sink in. You don't want to give up your worldly ways. Well, you can't straddle the fence either. You're either all the way in or all the way out. Speaking from experience, if you choose to go your way, He will bring you right back to Him.

So, you might as well tap out and submit. When God shows you the plan for your life, there is no rescinding the offer. He wants it to start taking place now because He knows the time has come and you are ready for it now. He knows your DNA makeup. He knows what you will become. You're viewing it all from your point of view when He didn't ask for your opinion. It's time for His will to be done.

You have now been called to do a mission for God. He has a purpose in mind and you are the "chosen" one. That means God has already equipped you with the artillery needed to complete the mission. When things are thrown at you along the way in with you view them as harm, God already has it covered. You are on assignment for Him. There will be times you may look like a fool fulfilling God's plan for your life but you must stay submitted to the plan. The purpose alone should provide you with intestinal fortitude. There is nothing to be afraid of. God's plan for you is to better YOU through HIM. So what if it has caused you to correct your worldly ways. You will become a better person as a result of it. You asked for it and He has shown it to you. Now submit to it!

## *When Okay Isn't Good Enough*

You ever get to the point in life when everything appears to be okay but there's still something inside of you insisting that it isn't? It's like you work and work to get to a certain point in life but you're not satisfied. Something inside of you asks, "Is this it?" "Is this what I've been working my tail off for all of my life?" Whether it be getting through college or getting that promotion you've so desperately wanted. After all of your hard work the satisfaction of completion could become melancholy. You ever get to the point when you're stuck in the middle? You're stuck in the middle of satisfaction and progress.

It reminds me of the days of driving down the freeway and smelling something awfully pungent. I was younger then and didn't know what the smell was. It smelled as though I had driven past a sewer plant. As I got older, I came to realize what that smell was and what had caused it. That portion of the freeway was near water that had become stagnant. Have you ever smelled stagnant water? The smell could be a real eye opener. Using this from a metaphoric standpoint, let's apply this to real life. Let's reference the point in time in which one could feel as though they were stuck in between satisfaction and progress. This could be considered as a "stagnant" moment. It's not a pleasant place to be in and it could feel quite awkward.

It's almost as if life has lost its luster. You must not allow for yourself to fall victim to complacency. It's quite easy to do. Over one shoulder you may look back at all you've accomplished to date. On the flip side, you may look into the future at other potential goals. Complacency sets in when you think of all of the hard work involved to move forward in life and you get the impression that you've accomplished enough. You think back to all it took to get you where you are today. Yes, you may want the future success but you don't want the hard work that's associated with it. You must not let your past accomplishments lull your future to sleep.

**"For the waywardness of the simple will kill them, and the complacency of fools will destroy them." Proverbs 1:32 (NIV)**

I use the example of Michael Jordan. I speak of the Michael Jordan before the six rings. I speak of the Michael Jordan who had already been labeled as the best player in the NBA but still had no ring.

Jordan had the hottest sneaker in the stores and all sorts of accolades but no championship. He hadn't won a single trophy. The Chicago Bulls would get close each year but would taste defeat in the playoffs each year. Now ask yourself. If Michael Jordan had looked over his shoulder at all of his past accolades instead of looking forward where would he be? Would he have gotten the first championship ring? Would he have gone on to become what many say, the greatest player ever? Imagine if he had settled, become complacent, and retired satisfied. After all, he was very wealthy. The world would have been robbed of history in the making.

Apply this same logic to yourself. To become complacent is one of the most foolish things you could ever do. What gives you the right to say I've gained enough? There is nothing else out there for me to gain. That's foolish thinking. You should have forward thinking. You should always be in motion to better yourself because as soon as you think you're "it", that's when someone else will snatch what you had away from you. Never be satisfied! Never just settle!

### "Never be satisfied! Never just settle!"

Look back over your life and reflect on how many things you've lost because of complacency. If you may be having a bit of trouble visualizing, let me provide a few scenarios. Ever gotten a job title with a bit of power? Mentally, you feel as though you've moved up in the world so you can ease up and relax a bit. You've put the car into cruise control for the remainder of the trip. Well, while you were on cruise control, you failed to notice the new person in your department. You figure, they're new so they're no threat. Weeks go by and months go by. You've made it to the top so you figure schooling and classes are of no use to you.

The new person has been taking classes and will finish college soon. A year or so goes by and you're called into the office to meet your new boss. Yes, you've guessed it. It's the new person in your department from about a year ago. They're now your new boss because you failed to better yourself and became complacent. You became stuck in your past successes. If you had managed to stay sharp and up on things with the proper training, you would have been in that position but you didn't. Past successes are for that point and time period only. They don't keep up with the times and they don't update themselves. You have to achieve success with the times and leave the past where it is, in the past.

### "Past successes are for that point and time period only."

How many of you are in relationships? How many disagreements have you had with your spouse because you went into something with an old and outdated mindset? You went into the situation doing something that may have worked with them years ago but they have evolved and now you've missed the mark. What may have gotten you out of the doghouse then doesn't get you out now. What may have charmed your spouse years ago doesn't charm them now. You have to re-invent yourself from time to time to keep things fresh. Change it up every now and then. Again, don't allow yourself to become complacent.

### "You have to re-invent yourself from time to time to keep things fresh."

The key to this whole thing is to not get to a point in life where you just settle. Your past successes will only take you so far and in this ever changing society we live in today, you'd better keep moving along with it in every aspect of your life. I may show my age but remember when we all thought the cassette tape was the next best thing and would never go anywhere? Now look where we are. CD's are almost obsolete. An iPod has made everything computer based. Change with the times. Keep thinking forward. Never become stagnant or you will start smelling as if you were stagnant. Your life will develop the stench of going nowhere and become boring.

I close by pointing back to one of the most famous incidents of being complacent. I'm referring to Leon Lett of the Dallas Cowboys during the Cowboy's hay day in the 90's. In short, Leon Lett had recovered a fumble and began rumbling towards the end zone for a touchdown. There was nothing but opportunity in front of Leon and his goal which was the end zone. Well, just as Leon Lett got around the 10 yard line, he let up and began to show boat.

He was so busy celebrating, that he failed to see the other team's wide receiver lurking. Right before Leon got to the touchdown, the other player knocked the ball out of his hands leaving the potential touchdown void. Prime example: Never become complacent! Dwelling in your past successes will leave you clinging to them as the world passes you by. Position yourself where you can grow. Complacency stunts growth! Remember that!

## *Outgrowing Your Circle*

    Have you ever felt like you were different than your peers? No, I don't mean in an arrogant way. I mean have you ever been around your peers and felt out of place? Have you ever had this nagging feeling inside of you telling you that you were called to do something great? You really can't explain what it is but you know it's there. You have a feeling you're going to finish your life in greatness.

Well, what goes through your mind when you find yourself in the middle of the room with your best friends holding a conversation and it does nothing for you? You're there listening to them talk about their struggles and complaints but they are not doing anything about it. Judging from their conversation, they don't plan to do anything about it either. They seem to get more enjoyment out of hearing themselves talk about their short comings rather than figuring out a way to correct them. The more you listen to them, the more you realize they are "talkers" and not "doers."

If you've ever had this experience you know what I speak of. You suddenly realize that your current circle is not where you belong if you want to chase those voices that have been calling you into greatness. I once heard that if you're the smartest one in your circle, then you're in the wrong circle. You need to be around people that stimulate your mind and not people who make you feel guilty about your mind set. They are content where they are in their lives. Remove yourself from them temporarily or permanently in order to position you further in the proper direction. They will be okay. The longer you waste time being in an unchallenging circle, the more time you are wasting away.

### "If you're the smartest one in your circle, then you're in the wrong circle."

It seems like we're always seeing someone that has become successful on the television and we find ourselves saying, "I knew them." Well, it's about time for your peers to say the same about you! Leave the rift raft behind and satisfy that burning desire inside of you that has been bugging you for years. You know where you are headed, don't let anyone deter you from getting there. Come to yourself and say, "Why am I here, hanging out with them?" "I deserve better than this." Why am I lowering MY standards to fit in when I should be exposing myself to a bigger and better crowd? You don't know the opportunities that are right around you because you never had the confidence to step outside of you current circle. You ever hear about how God brings people into your life for a reason? How do you think that happens a lot of times? Yes, you've guessed it. You could have this awesome vision inside of you to open up a chain of clothing stores. You think Willie and Fred at the liquor store have the resources or insight that you need in order to put your vision into motion? Not really.

> **"Leave the rift raft behind and satisfy that burning desire inside of you that has been bugging you for years."**

The key is to be in stimulating company. Put yourself in the company of those that are trying to be successful or have already achieved that pentacle in their lives. Put yourself in the presence of those that have similar interests as yours. How can you learn to be a success if you're around people who are not successful themselves? You're only as good as what you know, so make a conscious effort to educate yourself. You do this through exposure. A great amount of your needed knowledge won't come from schooling or books, it will come through exposure. Seeing and hearing may prove to be your biggest teachers.

> **"You're only as good as what you know, so make a conscious effort to educate yourself."**

What good is a talent or dream if you only put it on display inside of your under achieving circle? Hanging around talking about your past successes and your current struggles is not going to help you move forward. Step outside that small box! You wonder what highly successful people do? They position themselves around other highly successful people and they network with them. If you ever have the opportunity, step outside of the circle that you've outgrown and step into an intellectual circle. Just sit back and listen.

See what little tips you can pick up along the way so that you can apply them toward your upcoming success. You might even pick up a new dialect along the way. It'll be great to finally get a chance to use those complex words you were forced to study back in grade school. You might get the latest stock tips or be invited into a prestigious club that has a lot of connections. There are several things that could take place as long as you are willing to step outside of your circle. Expose yourself to the available resources that are out there waiting for you. You just have to be receptive and available to receive them! Position yourself into the proper circle!

## *The Pruning Process*

The act of pruning is a horticultural practice involving the selective removal of parts of a plant, such as branches, buds, or roots. Reasons to prune plants include deadwood removal, shaping by controlling or directing growth, improving or maintaining health, reducing risk from falling branches, increasing the yield or quality of flowers and fruits. The practice of pruning entails targeted removal of diseased, damaged, dead, non-productive, structurally unsound, or otherwise unwanted tissue from crop and landscape plants.

Have you ever gone out back of your home and pruned a tree? Perhaps you were out mowing the lawn and there were a couple of branches hanging that irritated the lights out of you. You had to get rid of them because they were in the way. Maybe they were hanging over the house damaging your roof in a major way. I titled this, "The Pruning Process" because in order to be successful, you must prune along the way in order to achieve success or move forward in your life. In this chapter, I will be using the metaphor of pruning a tree and referencing how it could be applied to your own life. Please allow me a moment of your time to elaborate as I flip back and forth between the two. You ever notice how much better a tree looks when it has been pruned? It has a crisp and clean appearance to it. You need to do this when it comes to your current life and your future. You must remove all of the detrimental things that have no purpose in your life but to clutter your vision of where you are and where you would like to go.

> **"You must remove all of the detrimental things that have no purpose in your life but to clutter your vision of where you are and where you would like to go."**

First thing, is to find a place of reflection. It could be out on the back porch or the park, but make sure you're by yourself to allow you to reflect. Don't go into the back room of the house thinking you will be in peace while the kids are arguing in the background. You need a place of solitude and a bit of time to reflect on your life. Think about what you would like to accomplish in your lifetime. Next, think about the things that are slowing you down or distracting you from achieving those sought after accomplishments. No, don't go back into the house and put a for sale sign on the arguing kids. This is just a corrective process, not extermination. One thing about pruning is that you must plan ahead as to what branches will be cut lose and which ones will remain. Yes, you know where I'm going with this. You must plan ahead as to what needs to be cut out and what will remain in your life. It's not just a "what" either. It could easily be a "who" that needs to be cut lose.

> **"You must plan ahead as to what needs to be cut out and what will remain in your life."**

How can you cut some things lose in order to get to where you want to be? I will warn you that this may be one of the roughest processes you will ever go through. There will be things that are dear to you and there will be things that you've grown accustomed to that you will have to give up. There will be bad habits that you will have to give up also. Bad habits are very difficult to break but you must make up in your mind that your future is more important. You must take an honest look at yourself and say, "What I'm doing is not working." Once you've strategized and figured out what it is that's hurting you, eliminate it. Don't look back indecisively or you will surely delay what you're trying to accomplish and end up in the same continuous circle until you get fed up again. Stick to your guns.

## "Don't look back indecisively or you will surely delay what you're trying to accomplish."

You've now devised a viable game plan on how you're going to go about starting the process and what needs to be pruned. Follow your devised game plan. It will tell you what fits and what doesn't fit in your life. Laying your game plan or blueprint out on the table will give you a great understanding of how big the job of pruning will be. You'll get a clear understanding of who's the enemy or if it's the inner me. I must warn you! You may not like what you see when it comes to cleaning up yourself but since when is cleaning up the trash a glamorous job? Let's begin to prune!

## "You'll get a clear understanding of who's the enemy or if it's the inner me."

Some people start at the top, some start at the bottom. The starting point shouldn't be the area of focus. Your focus should be on the effectiveness. It's like a video game. Each branch is worth a certain amount of points. You should be going after the branches that are worth more. I must caution you! Stay out of the way of falling branches. This refers back to sticking with your game plan. A falling branch can hurt you if you're not clear of it. Some people will not accept the fact that you are cutting them free. They will call you names. They will make attempts to ruin your character. They will do everything in their power to stop you from moving further. KEEP GOING! Remember? Once a branch has been cut off it clears away the clutter and improves the appearance of the tree. Get where I'm going with this? Don't worry about pleasing THEM. If they were so important, they would've made the cut anyway! Hand them their pink slips! Wave "bye" at them! Tell them I'm focused on my future!

### "The starting point shouldn't be the area of focus. Your focus should be on the effectiveness."

Referring to the definition listed at the beginning of this chapter. Take note of a few things: pruning controls and directs growth, pruning maintains or improves health. You can relate pruning your life to a strainer, allowing only the things that are important to remain, while the access waste drips away. Meaning, through this corrective process, you now have your tight knit supporting cast around you. You're not surrounded by the naysayers anymore. Now, through this corrective process, you've corrected the toxic behavior that has held you back all of these years. You should be amazed at how much better you can see things now that the clutter in your life has been removed. It's as if you now see life in high-definition. Every day of your life without the clutter allows you to focus on what your life is all about. What you want out of it and how you will achieve it. You can do it if you don't look back.

Now, to the fun part! Like a man that has just finished pruning a tree. He climbs down the ladder and steps back away from the tree with his tool in hand. He looks the tree over and pats himself on the back. Mission accomplished. My goal has been completed. "I'm a success" he thinks to himself, as he retreats back to his quarters. For those of you that have completed this step, I'm sure you can relate. Though there will be trials through your pruning process, it will be rewarding in the end. So I say to you, "Let's go pruning!"

## *Bondage*

What has you enslaved or under constraint? What are the things you know, if only you could free yourself from its snare, would allow for you to become free? Whatever that "thing" may be, could have you in a state of bondage. Bondage could be defined as the state of being under the control of a force or the state of being enslaved or under constraint. Are you under the control of a force? Are you enslaved by something? What could you do away with to allow you to go further in life? We all have something in our lives that seems to hold us down like dead weight. The problem lies with recognizing what has you in a bind. Then, you must ask yourself if you really want to face up to what has you enslaved.

**"And *that* they may recover themselves out of the snare of the devil which had been taken captive by him at his will."**

**2 Timothy 2:26**

Though it may be a little scary, you must realize that whatever has you in bondage is nothing more than a spirit! It's a spirit that you must cast out in order to be free. You do want to be free don't you? Go into your bathroom, look at yourself in the mirror and tell yourself, "I am going to break free from this thing that has a hold of me." It's very reminiscent of an addict. Your body and mind craves something that you desperately want to get away from. It's just for some reason; you end up where you started. Similar to an addict, your chances of being reformed by an environmental change may be very minimal. The true reformative process takes place by reforming your mind. Are you willing to reform your mind?

## "The true reformative process takes place by reforming your mind."

Let's explore a few scenarios. Have you ever been in financial bondage? There is a spending spirit that is awfully hard to shake. There is a compulsive urge to spend no matter the means of how you've obtained it. Whether it is cash, debit, or credit card, you must spend. This urge to spend is slowly causing your life to spiral out of control. You have found yourself living check to check with nothing going into savings. Every little bit has to be spent. When your check has been spent, you then resort to charging up your credit cards to feed this spirit.

Now, you are left with maxed out credit cards and stuck wondering how you're going to pay them off. You get a paycheck but you can only pay the minimum balance due. There are so many scattered payments that you're just inching along to pay off your debts. You've allowed this spirit to destroy your finances and if you're in a relationship, possibly that too. You have been robbed of your financial freedom.

> **"But the LORD hath taken you, and brought you forth out of the iron furnace, *even* out of Egypt, to be unto him a people of inheritance, as *ye are* this day." Deuteronomy 4:20**

Have you ever been in mental bondage where it seems like there is a struggle for your mind? There is a spirit from within that has you tied up with so many issues that you find it hard to be mentally free. You're constantly tired and mentally drained. Your mind may consist of the biggest ideas and dreams but you can't seem to find the time to put them into motion. It could be your job or it could be your living situation. You could easily get the false sense that you're stuck. When it comes to mental bondage it may be challenging because you must first realize what it is. There are so many things going on in your mind that it may be difficult to find the source.

One thing is for sure. There has been a spirit assigned specifically to occupy your mind from doing the things you were meant to do. You ever notice how as soon as you have a great idea; your life turns upside down? You could have more stress on the job or stress at the house, but it increases in an attempt to keep you from that which is good.

**"The thief does not come except to steal, and to kill, and to destroy. I have come that they may have life, and that they may have it more abundantly."**

## John 10:10

Have you ever been associated with someone who covertly had a bond on you? For some reason you couldn't shake them. This is the friend that you knew wouldn't be anything in life, never tried to be anything in life, but you still hung out with. You've tried to separate yourself from them time after time but you found yourself calling them on the weekends to hang out. You convinced your mind that you had nothing to do. Something kept drawing you to them. Was it the thrill you were after? You knew their habits and how they hung out in the streets but you felt you should stay in contact with them anyway. For some reason, you felt that you needed to stay in touch with your street side. What happens when staying in touch with your street side catches up with you? You find yourself doing something that isn't you? It is immoral behavior but you press ahead and do it anyway.

Now you're in a period of denial because you can't believe what you just did. Remember that job you applied for a few weeks ago? They now want to hire you but now you're unable to pass a urine analysis? You're up the creek with no paddle. How could you possibly have let this happen? How could you be so stupid and do drugs when you knew you were applying for jobs? You weren't able to break the bond of someone who didn't have good intentions.

Have you ever been in a situation where your lust outweighed your morals and values? You've searched for an exit but your lust has taken over? How do you handle such a bond? You came across someone who fulfills your inner most desires. Sounds great right? Wrong! I have to laugh because I know some of you think there is nothing wrong with a lustful bond. Well, it is. I can safely say that some of you got married because of lustful bond or had kids because of it. Your interaction with this person was merely a spirit of lust and not morals. You were so occupied by what their body looked like that you failed to see the warning signs. Sound familiar to anyone?

> **"What causes fights and quarrels among you? Don't they come from your desires that battle within you?" James 4:1**

What has you in bondage? What has restricted you from doing the right things? Please remember, bondage is nothing but a spirit, a spirit that has to be cast out in order to be broken. I can't possibly sit here and say that it doesn't require sacrifice and that it's not hard, but it's worth it. Your freedom is worth it! Imagine what you could be doing or how far you could go if there was nothing holding you down. Imagine how far along in life you could've been if you hadn't been bound in your past. I have to ask, "Was it worth it?"

Whatever you did as a result of being bound "Was it worth it?" Buying that item from the store, "Did it satisfy every desire?" Two or three hours of being high, "Was it worth not getting the job you wanted?" Thirty minutes of lustful bliss, "Were you better off?" Don't you want to live a limitless life? Don't you want to accomplish your goals in life? So you must ask yourself, "Do I even want to be broken from it or will I continue to drown in the ocean of mediocrity?" Break the chains! Take control of your life!

## *Psalms 1:1-3*

**To the men out there:**

Please take this as a word of encouragement. Although it may be rough on your path to your divine purpose, remember these words. I write this in hopes that it be a viable reference in a time of need.

## The Way of the Righteous and the End of the Ungodly

[1] Blessed *is* the man
    Who walks not in the counsel of the ungodly,
    Nor stands in the path of sinners,
    Nor sits in the seat of the scornful;

[2] But his delight *is* in the law of the LORD,
    and in His law he meditates day and night.

Blessed is the man who delights in the Lord.

[3] He shall be like a tree
    Planted by the rivers of water,
    that brings forth its fruit in its season,
    whose leaf also shall not wither;
    and whatever he does shall prosper.

I conclude by saying to the men out there who may have said they don't know exactly how to go about being successful. Like Nike, "Just do it." Once you jump out there and do what's in your heart ask God to bless it. You have to provide something for him to bless. Yes, there will be a LOT of work that needs to be done on your part but you must remain diligent in your approach.

Don't give up and don't let anything or anyone deter you from what you've always wanted to do. You know there's something in your heart that has been weighing on you for years now. Just do it! The time is now! He will not allow for you to wither. Just place yourself in the proper environment which will provide nourishment and when your season comes............be fruitful my man!

Grace! Peace! And Prosperity!

## *Adversity*

**"And we know that in all things God works for the good of those who love him, who have been called according to his purpose."
Romans 8:28**

I wanted to take the time to provide a bit of encouragement. We all know that life is full of ups and downs but we must see it as just that. You will have down moments and you will have moments when you're sky high. Simply knowing that life will fluctuate should give you a balanced outlook on life. You should know that life is going to test you. Life is going to grant you a bit of happiness at times and a bit of frustration at times.

**"Simply knowing that life fluctuates should give you a balanced outlook on life."**

The key is to transform or re-program your mind. Coming to this realization could take you a long way. Let me use a cliché phrase that I'm sure most of you have heard once before. "There are three stages when it comes to a storm. Either you're headed into a storm. You're in the middle of a storm or you're coming out of a storm." Let's discuss.

> **"There are three stages when it comes to a storm. Either you're headed into a storm. You're in the middle of a storm or you're coming out of a storm."**

When you're travelling on the road and see a storm approaching, what normally goes through your mind? The normal reaction has to do with a bit of worrying. You may worry about how soon it will be before you get to the storm. You may worry about how bad the storm will be. It's almost as if you brace yourself for what's about to come.

How many of you have shared these thoughts in your everyday life when you knew a storm was about to hit? It may have been a financial hit you knew was on its way or a bit of personal trouble headed your way. You saw the trouble approaching and you braced yourself with, "What am I going to do now?"

Now you are face to face with the approaching storm and you're about to enter the wall of showers. How do you react when the storm that you knew would be approaching has finally come? You are now forced to heighten your sense of focus. Here's where I want to rest a bit. What do you heighten your sense of focus on when in a storm? Are you focused on running for cover or do you shift your focus on getting through the storm? I must ask, "How do you handle storms when you're face to face with them?" Are you the type of person that says the storm is too much to bear and pulls over? The type of person that waits under the bridge for minutes, sometimes hours, making no progress towards their destination? Are you content with allowing the storm to have its way with you, as you cower under a safe haven?

If this is you, bind that cowering spirit in the name of Jesus! Don't let the storms you encounter in your life intimidate you into cowering and taking cover. If you want something badly enough you must square up on it and tackle it head on. We've heard the phrase, "If you don't like it, fix it." Don't settle for what the storm has presented you. You can get through it!

Remember, there's always a solution to a problem. You just have to apply yourself and work at finding it. That's the attitude you should have. You should have the mindset that through hell or high water, I'm going to keep pushing forward! The type of person that says, "I have a destination to get to and no devil in hell is going to stop me from getting to my destination!" Look the storm in its eyes, grit your teeth, and keep pushing forward!

Getting to your destination in life will require tenacity and personal drive. You can't expect anything good to happen to you by hiding and progress can't be made standing still. In life, no one is going to just knock on the door and hand anything to you. It's all about transforming your mind. Stop the attitude of expecting everything and being fearful of forward progress. Remove your hand from being out and use it to pull yourself upward. Get mad if you have to. Either way, keep moving! Now that you have gotten angry at your current situation, you should now be ready to fight the storm with pit bull tenacity.

You have been driving through the storm clutching the steering wheel while the windshield wipers have been knocking off the drops of adversity. You now realize that storms are not forever. Though intimidating, they only last a while. You can literally see the dry line where the storm will end. You now see that no matter how big the storm, it has to be an ending as you breathe a sigh of relief.

Warning! This is when most people let up. When the end is approaching and in their crosshairs they let off of the gas. When you see daylight and the end quickly approaching, you're to do one thing. Speed up! Why, you ask? Satisfaction comes at the ending. Like an Olympic sprinter dashing to the finish line, lean forward when you get to the tape. Though the storm may have caused you to slow down a bit out of caution, it was only for a short while and it wasn't meant to deter you.

The evidence is in the end of the storm when you come out. You look up at the sky out of thankfulness and what do you see? As beautiful as ever, you see a rainbow. A depiction of God letting you know that beauty can come out of adversity. I get mad at myself at times when I think of how adversity had robbed me in my past. The times of how the thought of adversity had me flinching and taking detours around the storm, adding time to my trips.

The silly thing, it was only a storm. Had I only put my head down, grit my teeth and went in head first, I would have seen it clearly. When I think about the moments of how the thought of adversity stunted my growth as a man or how the thought of adversity slowed my progress of finding my true purpose (destiny) in life, it angers me. The funny thing………………had I gone through the storm, I would have seen that God was there all along. He just had to test my will by putting a storm in the way of my destination to see how I would react.

# Men Cry in the Dark

How I arrived at the name of this chapter was through a revelation process. I went and saw the stage play, "Men Cry in the Dark" several years ago. It turned out to be pretty good but originally, I never got the just of the title. I think I took it as the obvious at the time. I felt, "Okay, no big deal." Of course, men don't want to be called weak, so we hide our emotions. If we do find ourselves getting emotional, we do it where no one else could see. I wrote it off and carried on with my life. It wasn't until later in my life that this topic started to resonate with me.

I would partake in several conversations or just overhear women conversing about their male counterparts. So, I wrote a post regarding a similar topic, "A man crying in front of his woman." I received several intriguing responses. I decided to take the topic a step further by performing this research face to face with several women for their take on the subject matter. I still came away a bit astonished. I've heard several women claim they wanted a man that was not afraid to display his emotional side but my research revealed a different factuality.

This does not speak for all women, but quite a few of them felt as if a man crying in front of them demonstrated a huge sign of weakness. I received feedback from several women affirming that they would actually lose a bit of respect for their man if he cried in front of them. I always thought it would be the total opposite but it was brought to my attention that it would make him appear as a "cry baby" and not the knight in shining armor that he had originally depicted.

I guess that goes to show the high standards that a man is held to when it comes to his emotions. You could be forced to limit what emotions could be revealed. It's almost as if being a man means you could reveal some emotions externally but not the deep ones. You can't threaten your image. Revealing your insecurities will make you appear weak right? Not exactly, but I must pose the question, "If we may be forced to absorb our deeper emotions, where do we conceal them?" I'll let you ponder on that a bit.

Let's explore a bit profoundly. In life, you will eventually come face to face with a disheartening situation that will actuate your softer emotions. There are going to be moments in your life that literally break you down. In short, there may be instances that literally make you cry. With a man, the crying may not take place externally but internally. This could easily be a result due to the emotional standards that have been placed upon him. Let me explain a bit further. Have you ever experienced a situation that internally ripped you to shreds? Maybe you've lost a loved one or experienced heartache with someone dear to you. You were so hurt by it but the testosterone pumping through your veins would not allow for you to shed a tear? How did you handle it? Did you find yourself in a state of confusion, not knowing how to get the pain out? Let's put this into perspective when it comes to the title of the play, along with our everyday lives.

I allude that the "dark" in the title where a man cries could be represented as the inside of a man's body, not a room with the lights off. I speak of the dark chamber that several men possess which has been buried deep within their bodies. I refer to it as a chamber because this is the very place where heartaches and failures dwell. This is the place that a man may be ashamed to let anyone view or see, including his spouse. When a man goes through a tough issue or rough patch in his life, he may process it for a diminutive amount of time and then ship it back to his own personal dark chamber.

Why would a man possibly store his innermost emotions in a dark chamber within instead of displaying it outwardly? Where could this behavior possibly have come from? I take you back to your younger years. For those that had a father figure around, how many times were you told to stop crying and tough it out when you were younger? You were told, "Be a man!"

How many times did your family go through a rough situation and when you viewed your father, he was steadfast in his demeanor? Your father knew the whole family would be looking to him as the source of strength so naturally, had to be the rock. Though the moment was painful for him as well, he couldn't bear to let the rest of the family in on his travail. Your father had to process what had taken place and tuck it away deep inside his own dark chamber. Tucking it away allowed for him to place it as far away as possible.

Take a moment and fast forward to the present. Do you find yourself emulating what you saw your father do? Did any of his behavioral traits during travail stay with you into your manhood? What teachings do your refer back to when faced with a tough situation? There may have been traits passed down to you from generation to generation without your knowledge. When a tough situation comes before you. You may process it for a moment and then tuck it deep within. All of this to remain steadfast in your demeanor like your father.

Let's discuss briefly what takes place during the process of tucking those heavy emotions into your chamber. What may take place is a battle internally between your mannish pride and your emotions. Your mannish pride is reverting back to those words "man up" you grew up hearing. Your emotional side is trying to explain to your brain that this really does hurt emotionally. What are you going to do? Will you allow for your emotions to be written all over your face and get the best of you or will you suck it up and be strong?

Several times we allow our mannish pride to win this battle. Why, you ask? It's because you're a man and as a man, we can have a hard time allowing something to get the upper hand on us. Competition appears to be embedded in the majority of us, which makes it difficult for us to display any weaknesses. It's the revving your engine at the red light when next to another car syndrome.

With all of that being said, when dealing with something that is highly disheartening, the news may be received, processed and shipped back to your dark chamber. The deeper you bury it, the less you have to deal with it emotionally. The way you see it, if you could just put your hurts out of sight and mind, the better chance you could stand with your head held high though you have just been severely wounded.

**"The deeper you bury it, the less you have to deal with it emotionally."**

As men, we could talk a good game and maintain a great poker face but internally we could be quite fragile, though we may not want to admit it. Your audience may never become exposed to your concealed emotions. Warning! Though you may have an innate ability to process disheartening information quickly and store it into your dark chamber, the time will come when it resurfaces. To some it may take a few days, maybe a few years, but it will ultimately take its toll.

Through a grueling maturation process, I had to realize that if I didn't find an outlet for the hurtful things in my dark chamber, I would self-implode. I realized that I couldn't contain all of the pain and heartache I had encountered in my life forever. This would have me eventually keeling over from cardiac arrest. To be quite honest, I didn't know that I had a God that I could cast all of my hurts upon. I didn't realize that He wouldn't allow for anything to happen to me that I couldn't handle. They were all just tests bringing me closer to Him if I only allowed myself to be open to what He was trying to tell me. To think, I foolishly thought that I was strong enough to bare it all on my own shoulders without His help.

I'm sadly reminded of what those actions could do to me, as I mourn the loss of my grandfather and my father. Both passed away due to stress related heart attacks. I grew up watching my father stand strong in the gap as pain struck him and my family, not knowing how fragile he was becoming from tucking the pain away in his dark chamber. Who knew but God of the fatal outcome? I must admit that I find myself at times going down the same path. I would stand pat not giving ground to anyone who could possibly be within viewing distance of my travail. Hours and sometimes days would go by with me holding everything inside. What I have now come to realize is through prayer, He will envelope me with a comforting spirit. At times it's a feeling of chilled water through my veins. It's Him letting me know to calm down. He has it covered. Since I have taken the time to seek Him, He has taken the time to reveal to me peace of mind and a peaceful spirit.

What I have revealed to you, the reader, is that no matter what the pain is or whatever the hurt may be, cast it on God. All of those things that you may be ashamed to let anyone know of, cast them on God. I know, we've all messed up big time but there is nothing too big for Him. No, this isn't an altar call; this is a "man check." Though we may not be able to tell our women the things we may have done in private or even our private emotions, let God be your psychiatrist. After all, He's God, not some human being. He's on a higher playing field. I'm passionate about this because I have lost loved ones in the process from the "crying in the dark." For those of you that have a tendency to hold it all in, it's time to break the cycle while you can. Open your chamber to God. Stop the internal withering and live!

## *Let It Go!*

**"Nothing outside a man can make him "unclean" by going into him. Rather, it is what comes out of a man that makes him "unclean."
Mark 7:15-16**

I wanted to take a moment to address an issue that many men are facing in today's society. The issue I'm referring to is the acknowledgement of when to let certain things go. As long as you're living and well, there's one thing that you will continue to do and that's age. No matter how much you may not want to admit it, you're going to get older. There's no way around it. With age, wisdom should come. I hate to admit it but not all men have picked up on the wisdom portion. I'm alluding to the things they should do and the things they should not do at their age. Then again, maybe some men just don't want to acknowledge the fact that they are getting older.

**"With age, wisdom should come."**

There comes a time in a man's life when he should realize he's past his prime in certain areas. I'm still fairly a younger man in my 30's and I'm starting to put forth the wisdom that I've obtained over the years. I'm starting to piece together the things I should partake in and the things I should avoid because I just know better. Age and life's teachings have shown me that. As a man grows older and wiser, so should his environment which brings me to my first topic; environment.

**"As a man grows older and wiser, so should his environment."**

What is your environment like? Does it portray the knowledge and wisdom that you have acquired through life's teachings? I can tell you one thing. Hanging out in front of the local liquor store or neighborhood grocery is not a fruitful environment. If this applies, you owe it to yourself to be better than that. That is not the environment you were created to be in. Even if you're in a pretty stable situation you could stand to do a little better. I know if asked, the answer would be "yes" when it came to having a better life, so why not strive for better?

**"You owe it to yourself to be better than that."**

I know I've stated several times that your environment could play a huge part in the progression of your life and that's true. I also know that though challenging, you sometimes have to go against the grain to become better. You can't always go with the flow if you aspire to become a better man. Sometimes you must take a step back and evaluate your current surroundings. There should come a time when you must say, "I'm better than this!"

Your life long teachings and the wisdom acquired through maturity should allow you to "come to yourself" like the Prodigal Son (**Luke 15:11-32)** and return to your proper surroundings. What productivity will take place hanging on the street corners? What is there to gain? Is this where you would like to be for the rest of your life? I'm not suggesting that you leave your friends behind at all. What I am suggesting is that you go against the grain and limit your involvement in an attempt to become better.

There is no need to be in the streets partaking in such activities that make you appear street wise, especially in your upper age. It frustrates me to see so called "OG's" trying to be the neighborhood kingpin. It also frustrates me to go somewhere and I'm talking to older men who use the famous phrase, "In my day, I used to…….." Time is the one thing you can't take back, so why waste it on foolishness? Yes, we all were once younger and did foolish things, but there must come a time when you put the foolishness behind.

**"Go against the grain and limit your involvement in an attempt to become better."**

It's not just the street corners. It's the strip clubs also. I maybe should have left that one out huh? Hey, it has to be addressed. I have a few associates that spend the majority of their evenings hanging out in the strip clubs. Don't get me wrong, I love women as much as the next man but what productivity comes out of it? Going somewhere and handing a woman my hard earned money is just not that productive to me. Women in strip clubs are there to sell you one thing which is a "dream." Sell you a visual. The majority of the times you don't leave with her and you end up with your wallet a bit lighter. Let it go!

I would now like to hang my hat on the introducing scripture for a moment. "Nothing outside a man can make him "unclean" by going into him. Rather, it is what comes out of a man that makes him "unclean." (Mark 7:15-16) It suggests, what comes into you does not corrupt you, what you put out does. Meaning, you could be in the presence of nonsense and not become corrupted. You are only corrupted when you allow what is inside of you to come out distorted and twisted. I suggest that if you don't place yourself in that type of environment in the first place, you won't be tempted. So, if you find yourself in this type of environment, run. Run away as far as you can.

> **"You are corrupt when you allow what is inside of you to come out distorted and twisted."**

Let's address those of you that feel as if they have something to prove when it comes to today's youth. If you're in your later years, please present yourself as such. Don't make dubious efforts to fit in. You're not a teenager or in your 20's anymore. It's time to start acting your age. You have nothing to prove to today's youth nor do several of them really care. If the youthful circle you hang around doesn't look up to you as a role model, then you're probably viewed as a has been. They should revere you, not laugh at you.

Here's a mental note. You know you're in the wrong era when you can't relate to what the youth is doing anymore. My advice to you is to move on to more relative environments. Again, you have nothing to prove. You must realize that your time has come to an end in that particular arena. You had your fun in your heyday.

## "You know you're in the wrong era when you can't relate to what the youth is doing anymore."

To the grown man that still wants to be in player mode, this falls back to the strip club scenario. The young lady that you are chasing is there to provide a pipe dream. You're steady shoveling out cash to make it appear as though you still have it, while all along she's taking your cash. You get what? A glimpse of how she looks half naked. Yeah, you're the man, while you are funding her and her true love, which is her man at home. Wake up! Do away with the "sugar daddy" syndrome. Believe me when I say that it's hard to give it up. Lord knows it is! I too find it hard at times but as you become older and wiser you must look forward to building something positive for your future.

Trying to hold on to the player persona will leave you old and alone. You'll realize that when you get up in age, the women in your age group are looking to settle down. Any woman looking to settle down is not going to put up with your foolishness for too long. You won't be able to straddle the fence with them. If you can't show commitment, they're gone. So again, stop the adolescent behavior and get you a good woman by your side. At least there, you won't have to worry about being sold a pipe dream.

> **"As you become older and wiser you must look forward to building something positive for your future."**

You know what? I ran across a situation recently that caught me off guard. It made me truly realize that I must be moving in the right direction. I ran across a married associate of mine that asked where I hung out. I didn't find anything alarming at the time. What caught me by surprise was that he asked if there were any women there. He went on to explain how he had an apartment across town and his wife didn't have a clue.

What got me was the fact that he was acting nonchalantly as if he were still single. I thought to myself, why not just be single if you're going to run around and chase these young girls? Better yet, "Why aren't you at home with your wife?" You have an assumingly good woman at home but you're out chasing the cat, being a dog. Now, if your woman isn't worth it, cut her loose but don't keep running around trying to have your cake and eat it too. It will all come back and bite you. When you least expect it, you will become too confident and make a mistake. Two things most likely will happen. Either you will get caught in the act with the other woman or your wife will become lonely and takes matters into her own hands. When you walk in to see your wife naked in the bed with another man, what can you say? You can't be a hypocrite and be mad. You were having your fun and now she's having hers. It's a tough pill to swallow but it happens every day.

I would also like to touch on a few more topics. One of them is appearance. It should be in your earlier years but definitely in your older years when you realize how to present yourself in public for the proper occasion. I can understand dressing down when off work and making a quick run to the store but when you have an engagement, step it up a bit appearance wise. Wearing jerseys and tennis shoes to a banquet just don't cut it.

Also, the way you appear DOES matter when it comes to the respect you receive. I perform self-research all of the time to see the differences. When I go to the store on my lunch hour in my slacks and dress shirt, I command respect so that's what I receive. When I'm off work and need to run somewhere, I like to dress down and relax.

It's night and day. Even the cop at the entrance views me differently. Yes, I know you shouldn't care about what others think but next time you walk into a store and need assistance, tell me what type of service you receive. This doesn't just pertain to attire.

Dialect does play a huge part in it as well. I never will forget when I heard all of the hype about a well-known celebrity when she stepped on the scene. I was dying to get a glimpse of this beauty. I finally got my chance to see her on a talk show. I waited patiently to see if her voice matched the Goddess of a body she had. When she opened her mouth and spoke, I was a bit appalled. I can't express the things that went through my mind at the time.

So, your dialect could definitely make or break you. I'm not saying that you should sell out and be something you're not. What I AM saying is that you must learn how to be liquid when it comes to your dialect. Adjust to any given situation. For example: an interview. If you're trying to get a job, you can't walk in as if you're conversing with one of the guys. Present yourself in a grown manner. Leave the childish ways in the wind.

Letting go of your childish ways does not mean your life has come to an end nor does it mean the excitement has to be lost. All it means is that you make better and more precise decisions. Part of being a grown man and letting go of the childish things is commanding respect and giving respect when due. Taking care of your business and not playing around with your life. Positioning yourself around those who are trying to take care of their business. Being submitted to a concept. Frankly, just act your age and let go of the childish ways. I pray that this piece lands in the proper hands. I pray that this serves as a wake-up call to be a better person.

## *You Know Better*

These men are springs without water and mists driven by a storm. Blackest darkness is reserved for them. For their mouths empty, boastful words and, by appealing to the lustful desires of sinful human nature, they entice people who are just escaping from those who live in error. They promise them freedom, while they themselves are slaves of depravity—for a man is a slave to whatever has mastered him. If they have escaped the corruption of the world by knowing our Lord and Savior Jesus Christ and are again entangled in it and overcome, they are worse off at the end than they were at the beginning. It would have been better for them not to have known the way of righteousness, than to have known it and then to turn their backs on the sacred command that was passed on to them. Of them the proverbs are true: "A dog returns to its vomit," and, "A sow that is washed goes back to her wallowing in the mud." - **2 Peter 2:17**

# My Pledge

I would like to conclude what I hope was an enjoyable, yet eye opening experience for you. I hope that this book reached you internally like no other has. I know that sometimes as a man, we have a hard time expressing our emotions or have a hard time wondering why we react a certain way to certain situations. I hope this book assisted you in answering some of those questions.

I wanted to offer a pledge to you that I will stand by as long as the good Lord provides me with the tools and insight. I pledge to you that I will continue to push myself in an attempt to get better so that I could enlighten the world at a higher level. I stand by my pledge by stating that HE is in ME and I will make every attempt not to manipulate but educate. I make a pledge to you that I will do my best to conduct myself as a man of God. Although I may fall short at times, I will still attempt perfection in HIS eyes. He's not finished with me yet.

## To the men that have come across this book:

I would like for you to make a pledge as well to better yourselves, to better your homes, to better our society, to better the future, and most importantly, to better yourselves in the eyes of God. Make a pledge to believe in YOURSELF.

The vision that was laid out for someone else was not tailor made for you. YOU have your own road map to follow. Stay on path. If you should ever make a wrong turn along the way, recalculate. Don't let anyone tell you that you can't do it because you CAN. It's YOUR vision so manifest it. It just takes VISION, ACTION, FAITH, and watch GOD work.

I humbly thank you for sharing this venture with me. I enjoyed every minute of it in anticipation of presenting it to you.

*The Facets of Man*

*Volume I*

*The Building Blocks*

www.ingramcontent.com/pod-product-compliance
Lightning Source LLC
Chambersburg PA
CBHW051834090426
42736CB00011B/1794